幼保 英語検定

Pre-1級ワークブック

【編集】 一般社団法人 国際子育て人材支援機構（OBP）

kidsfore
キッズフォレグループ
ブックフォレ　　株式会社ブックフォレ

はじめに

本書は幼児教育・保育英語検定（以下、幼保英語検定といいます）準1級用の学習用教材です。

幼保英語検定は、出題範囲が幼児教育に関連している分野であるため、保育士・幼稚園教諭の方及びこれらの資格取得、分野への就職を考えている学生・外国人の方には、最適の英語検定です。

この検定は、文法や語彙力といった観点より「日常会話力」に重視している点で、日本のこれからの国際化に必要な「外国語の会話力」を習得する先鞭をつけた検定です。ぜひ、多くの方に受検頂き、「机上の英語力」、「話せない英語力」ではなく、「実践的な会話力」を身につけてください。

本書は、幼保英語の早期習得を目指し実践的な学習ができるように、3回分の問題を検定形式で掲載しています。

幼保英語検定の検定学習としては、一般社団法人幼児教育・保育英語検定協会の著書「幼保英語検定テキスト」で基礎を学習し、学習度合いの確認及び検定直前の実力確認用として、本書を活用ください。

目次

＊リスニング問題用音源は、こちらのホームページよりダウンロードをしてください。

https://bookfore.co.jp/glh/download/

幼児教育・保育英語検定
（略：幼保英語検定）とは

幼保英語検定は、幼稚園教諭及び保育士等幼児教育者のみならず、乳幼児保育に携わる方々が、幼稚園、こども園及び保育園等幼児教育施設等の乳幼児保育環境において、英語でのコミュニケーション力の習得状況を知り、さらに向上させることができる検定です。

乳幼児との会話、園内の教育・保育に焦点をあて、現場に即した実践英語を習得できることが大きな特色です。

園内教育・保育及び保護者との日常会話から連絡・交流に必要な題材まで、受検者の学習を考慮し工夫された内容になっており、楽しみながら知識を深められる構成となっています。「入門レベル」から責任者として活躍できる「専門レベル」までの 5 段階で構成されており、英語力の向上を実感できるだけではなく、資格を取得することで幼児教育、保育分野で幅広く活用でき、幼児教育、保育環境の国際的なグローバル化に対応できる実践的な英語力を段階に応じて有することが証明できます。

第1回　問題

時間	筆記（英作文含む）50分	リスニング　30分
問題数	筆記　40問　英作文　1問	リスニング　25問
点数	筆記　1問1点　英作文　10点	リスニング　1問2点
解答	筆記、リスニング	解答用紙（マークシート）
	英作文	英作文専用用紙

注意事項　　　この問題の複製（コピー）転用を禁じます。

Section I

A word or phrase is missing in each of the sentences. Select the best answer to complete the sentence.
Mark the number 1, 2, 3 or 4 on your answer sheet. (Please fill in the entire circle darkly and completely.)

Q.1　　（　　） we have 25 children enrolled in our nursery program, with a ratio of 1 teacher to 5 students.

1. Forthwith　　　　2. Straightaway　　　3. Currently　　　　4. Momentarily

Q.2　　Okay children, we are getting ready to make our drive to the aquarium. Please (　　) your seatbelts before we leave.

1. clasp　　　　　2. buckle　　　　　3. harness　　　　4. clip

Q.3　　I'm so sorry I was late! The traffic was (　　) this morning!

1. toe to toe　　　2. neck and neck　　3. back to back　　4. bumper to bumper

Q.4　　Is it still raining out there? Not really, just a bit (　　).

1. misty　　　　　2. humidity　　　　3. hail　　　　　4. downpour

Q.5　　Tomorrow we are expecting a lot of snow, so children are expected to (　　) before coming to school.

1. shovel their driveway
2. have a snowball fight
3. wear hats and gloves
4. slip on the ice

8

 Section I

Q.6　Blow out your candles and keep your wish to yourself otherwise it may not (　　).

1. come out　　　　2. blossom　　　　3. come true　　　　4. grow

Q.7　Tomorrow night we will be holding a parent development session. (　　) is required for all parents. See you tomorrow night!

1. Encouragement　　2. Absence　　　　3. Engagement　　　　4. Participation

Q.8　The (　　) for this year's school play has been selected. They are all good actors.

1. roster　　　　　2. cast　　　　　　3. attendance　　　　4. outline

Q.9-Q.10 Choose the best answer from the choices below the question.

Q.9　What does the expression "it slipped my mind" mean?

1. to have forgotten something
2. to have become confused
3. to have not understood
4. to become nervous

Q.10　What does it mean when we say an illness is "going around".

1. That the illness isn't particularly contagious.
2. That many people have be catching the illness.
3. The illness mostly affects travelers.
4. The illness cannot be stopped by preventative medicine.

Section II

Dialogues-A word or phrase is missing in each of the sentences. Select the best answer to complete the sentence. Mark the number 1, 2, 3 or 4 on your answer sheet. (Please fill in the entire circle darkly and completely.)

Q.11-Q.20 Read the two dialogues below and fill in the blanks with the best word or phrase below the dialogue.

Dialogue 1   Conversation between two parents, Mariko and Judy

Mariko: Hey Judy, are you excited for the children's play this year?

Judy: I'm looking forward to it, but I am a bit worried about making Conner's (Q.11). He is playing a bird.

Mariko: Well I'd be happy to (Q.12) if you like. I've been making these things for years now.

Judy: Wow! That would be wonderful. Thanks so much for (Q.13). It really means a lot.

Mariko: No problem. For me, I am kind of nervous about Momoka's speaking. She has so many (Q.14) to remember.

Judy: I totally understand. Conner has been having butterflies in his stomach about his speaking role.

Mariko: Yeah, it really is tough on kids, but I feel like it builds up their leadership skills.

Judy: Yeah you are right. Well the good news is there are still several (Q.15) before the actual play.

Mariko: Exactly! Still lots of practice time to go. Let's cross our fingers!

Q.11	1. wardrobe	2. fashion	3. uniform	4. costume
Q.12	1. look out	2. help out	3. try out	4. guidance
Q.13	1. proposing	2. suggesting	3. volunteering	4. enlisting
Q.14	1. lines	2. stanzas	3. paragraphs	4. speeches
Q.15	1. workouts	2. rehearsals	3. retellings	4. performances

Section II

Dialogue 2　　　Phone conversation between a parent and the preschool director

Parent:　Thank you so much for (Q.16) to meet me on such short notice.

Director:　Sure, what seems to be the trouble? I heard you had some issue with our Setsubun celebration last week.

Parent:　Yes, even since the festival my child hasn't been able to sleep. The teacher playing the oni (Q.17) so loudly that my child is having nightmares.

Director:　I see, I am very sorry to hear that your child had such a negative experience.

Parent:　Don't get me wrong, I appreciate your efforts to teach Japanese culture, but I just hate to see my child so (Q.18) school.

Director:　Please rest assured that I will discuss this matter with all teachers and I promise we will adjust our approach (Q.19) for next year's event.

Parent:　Thank you so much. I am (Q.20) to hear that.

Director:　Okay, see you tomorrow morning.

Q.16　　1. complying　　　2. denying　　　　3. resisting　　　4. agreeing

Q.17　　1. elevated their voice
　　　　2. sounded their voice
　　　　3. raised their voice
　　　　4. heightened

Q.18　　1. burnt out about
　　　　2. put out about
　　　　3. stressed out about
　　　　4. dropped out about

Q.19　　1. correspondingly　　2. accordingly　　　3. fixability　　　4. unsuitably

Q.20　　1. relieved　　　　2. distraught　　　3. pacified　　　4. alleviated

Section III

In this section of the test you will read 2 passages. The first passage is followed by 15 questions related to information or vocabulary in the reading passage. The second passage is followed by 10 questions. Please choose the best answer for each question.

Reading Passage 1 Q.21-Q.35　　Empathy: Teaching Children to Value Those Around Them

Empathy is one of those strange (Q.21). Something almost everyone wants, but few know how to truly give or receive it. In a world where self-gratification is (Q.22), empathy is in short supply, but high demand. This is all the more reason to teach the next (Q.23) what it means to have empathy for those around them.

Many people confuse sympathy and empathy, but they are two distinct values. Empathy is more than that. Not only is it the ability to recognize how someone feels, but also to value and respect the feelings of another person. It means (Q.24) others with kindness, dignity, and understanding.

While some children are gifted with naturally kind hearts, (Q.25) kids need to see empathy modeled by the adults around them. (Q.26) the way parents relate to their children. Parents who show an interest in the things that matter to their kids and respond to emotions in a positive and caring way are teaching the skill of empathy.

When children have their emotional needs met, they learn how to meet the emotional needs of others. (Q.27) when children's own emotional needs are met. **An empty jug cannot fill a cup.** Many adults find it hard to talk about emotional needs or anything related to emotions, but it's vital that adults work past this discomfort and talk to kids about emotions and how other people experience them. Give their emotions names (for example, jealousy, anger, and love) and teach them that these are normal. Talk to them about how to handle emotions in a positive way and point out situations where other people are experiencing emotions. (Q.28) a real life example to model what you are teaching. Look for situations that affect another person and talk to your kids about what it means to the people involved and how they might feel. For example, if you see an ambulance speed past, talk about how the family members of the sick person (Q.29).

Younger kids in particular love to (Q.30) that they are someone or something else. You can use these fun times for teaching empathy. Get your kids playing the role of another person. This might be a character in a book or on TV, or even someone you know who has been through a **significant** experience lately. You can act out the story together and ask your kids to stop and imagine how their character might have been feeling at any given moment. This will focus their attention on the emotions that another person might experience when in that situation. You can ask them to make faces that reflect the feelings of their character.

 Section III

(Q.34)

By raising your kids to understand and practice empathy, you're giving them the gift of giving. In a world where great emphasis is placed on looking out for your own interests, people who are givers are all too rare. But they are the ones who enjoy the greatest satisfaction from life, live the most meaningful lives, and enjoy more rewarding relationships. Teaching your kids empathy is a worthwhile investment for their own futures and for the world they will inhabit.

Q.21-Q.24 Please choose from the following words to fit the blanks for Q.21- Q.24 in the first paragraph. Choose from the list below.

1. generation   2. qualities   3. treating   4. emphasized

Q.25-Q.29 Please choose from following phrases to fit the blanks for Q.25-Q.29 in the second paragraph. Choose from the list below.

Q.25   1. contrary to belief   3. in most cases
        2. due to the fact   4. on the other hand

Q.26   1. However   3. As a general rule
        2. It begins with   4. Focusing on

Q.27   1. Starting from   3. At a time
        2. This can only be done   4. If and

Q.28   1. There is nothing like   3. Steering away from
        2. Carefully avoiding   4. Comparatively

Q.29   1. found that situation   3. are so unlucky
        2. could have avoided the situation   4. might be feeling

 Section III

Q.30-Q.35 Please choose the answer that best fits the question.

Q.30　　Choose from the list of words below that best fits the blank.

　　　　1. purport　　　　　2. reveal　　　　　3. deny　　　　　4. pretend

Q.31　　According to paragraphs 4 and 5, which of the following is NOT true about children learning empathy?

　　　　1. They must first have their emotional needs met.
　　　　2. Role-play is not an effective method to learn empathy.
　　　　3. Parents should teach the names of various emotions.
　　　　4. Making faces can help young children get in touch with emotions.

Q.32　　What does the sentence **an empty jug cannot fill a cup** mean, as it is used in paragraph 4?

　　　　1. Some people make poor teachers.
　　　　2. Some people have hollow and empty lives.
　　　　3. You cannot give what you do not have.
　　　　4. Children simply do not have enough knowledge to mentor.

Q.33　　Which of the following is a synonym for **significant** as it is used in paragraph 5?

　　　　1. trivial　　　　　2. traumatic　　　　　3. important　　　　　4. minor

 Section III

Q.34　What is the correct order of the words deleted from paragraph 6?
　　　（＊答えの選択肢の文頭は小文字で記載しています）

　　　　1. the　　　　　　2. of　　　　　　3. you're　　　　4. gift
　　　　5. giving　　　　6. compassion

　　　　1.　1-3-4-5-6-2　　　　　　　3.　6-1-2-4-5-3
　　　　2.　2-3-1-4-5-6　　　　　　　4.　3-5-1-4-2-6

Q.35　According to the passage, what is a benefit of children practicing empathy?

　　　　1. They will live more meaningful lives.
　　　　2. It will make them closer to their parents.
　　　　3. They will no longer confuse empathy and sympathy.
　　　　4. They will value their teachers and mentors more.

 Section III

Reading Passage 2 Q.36-Q.40   A Letter from Kids Patio Preschool Regarding Open House

Dear Kids Patio Families,

    We hope that you all are well. We are writing to (Q.36) you that Open House signups are now available. Open House will be held at Kids Patio from May 22nd - 26th. Open House is a week-long event held twice yearly where parents are able to sign up to come and (Q.37) their child's normal school day. A child's schooling is a major part of their life and growth that parents are unable to be a part of everyday. As parents this can be quite tough, as young children are learning and (Q.38) many new things each day. It's difficult to not be able to be there for some of those special moments.

    With this in mind, Open House at Kids Patio is designed to provide parents with an opportunity to gain a greater insight into this area of their child's life and development. We hope that parents will use this opportunity positively to observe this side of their child's life and to peak in on their development.

    Parents will be able to gain insight into how their children act and respond to their school development, as well as get a better idea of their child's normal school day and the types of activities that they do. While at the Open House feel free to involve yourself in your child's activities and do be aware of the fact that the presence of many families during the school day will change your child's behavior. Some children may act unusually shy, while others may cry out of anxiety due to wondering what all the changes are about. Nevertheless, we hope that you will be able to walk away from the Open House experience feeling proud of all that your children accomplish on a daily basis at Kids Patio.

    The signup sheet is located at the school entrance. Please be sure to sign up for the specific dates, times, and levels that you would like to attend. Each family is allowed to visit one day of their choice and all families are welcome to visit all levels in the school. We also encourage you to bring a family friend that you feel may be interest in Kids Patio's programs. Open House is also a unique opportunity for them to gain first-hand experience with our wonderful community.

    Signups for Open House will officially close on Friday, May 19th. We will be unable to accommodate any late sign ups, but please be sure to sign up before the due date. Thank you for your cooperation.

                  Sincerely,
                  Principal Yamada

 Section III

Q.36 -Q.38 Choose a word from the list below that best fits in the blank spaces in the sentences marked (Q.36), (Q.37) and (Q.38). One choice does not fit any of the blank spaces.

1. achieving   2. inform   3. observe   4. considered

Q.39   According to the letter parents are advised that their children's...

1. Learning may be stunted by their presence.
2. Schedule will be different than normal.
3. Friends are welcome to join them at school.
4. Behavior may be different than usual.

Q.40   According to the letter, which of the following is NOT an intended purpose of Open House?

1. To provide parents with insight into their child's school life.
2. To allow parents an opportunity to evaluate teachers.
3. To create an opportunity to peak in on their child's development.
4. To help parents feel a sense of pride for what their child accomplishes in school.

 Section IV

Writing

Ms.Suzuki:　　Hey are you going to the staff BBQ this Sunday?

Ms.Yamanaka:　I would love to. The weather looks like it's going to be beautiful, but I have a doctor's appointment at noon.

Ms. Suzuki:　　Don't worry just come after your doctor's appointment. We'll probably be there until 5 or 6pm anyway.

Ms. Yamanaka: You don't think Principal Yamada will mind if I show up late?

Ms. Suzuki:　　It's for a medical appointment, so I am sure he will understand. Then just bring a bottle of wine and all the teachers will forgive you for sure!

Ms. Yamanaka: (laughing) Great idea! A bottle of red it is! See you on Sunday.

Q.41　　In this section you will read a dialog. In 30-35 words, write a summary of the dialog you just read.

Evaluation points:

①Your answer will be evaluated for the correct use of grammar and sentence structure, proper spelling and punctuation. (Commas, periods and other punctuations are not included in the number of words.)

②The summary of the dialog needs to say:
1)What event is happening?
2)When is it happening?
3)What is Ms. Yamanaka's problem?

第1回　問題
Listening Test

準1級リスニングテストについて
（テスト開始までの一分間で下記をよく読んでください）

●このテストはSection IとSection IIにわかれています。

●放送の間、メモをとっても構いません。

●最後のQ.66の後、10秒するとテスト終了の合図がありますので、筆記用具を置いて答えの記入を
やめてください。

Section I (Q.42-Q.50)　　　　イラストを参考にしながら、対話を聞き、その質問に対して最も適切
　　　　　　　　　　　　　　な答えを1,2,3,4の中から一つ選ぶ形式です。
　　　　　　　　　　　　　　対話と質問は、1回ずつ放送されます。

Section II (Q.51-Q.66)　　　英文を聞き、最も適切な答えを1,2,3,4の中から一つ選ぶ形式です。英
　　　　　　　　　　　　　　文と答えは、1回ずつ放送されます。

　　無断転載・複写を禁じます

Section I

In this section of the test you will hear four dialogues. After each dialogue there are some questions. Choose the best answer from the list below the questions.

Dialogue 1 Q.42-Q.46

Q.42　Who was responsible for arranging the meeting between Principal Yamada and Ms. Yamanaka?

1.

2.

3.

4.

Q.43　What was Principal Yamada's issue with Ms. Yamanaka?

1.

2.

3.

4.

Q.44　Who is responsible for teacher scheduling?

1.

2.

3.

4.

Q.45　Why do you think Ms. Yamanaka is struggling with her role?

1.

2.

3.

4.

Q.46　　How did Principal Yamada solve Ms. Yamanaka's problem?

1.

2.

3.

4.

Dialogue 2 Q.47-Q.51

Q.47　　Why do you think Principal Yamada agreed to meet with Ms. Ishikawa after school hours?

1.

2.

3.

4.

Q.48　　What is Ms. Ishikawa's dilemma?

1.

2.

3.

4.

Q.49　　What is one of the Ishikawa's main concerns for Ayaka's elementary school?

1.

2.

3.

4.

Q.50　　How does Principal Yamada assist Ms. Ishikawa with her dilemma?

1.

2.

3.

4.

 Section II

Listening Passage 1 Q.51-Q.55

Removing the Bubble Wrap

Q.51　According to the passage overprotecting children has what effect?

1.

2.

3.

4.

Q.52　Which of the following was NOT suggested as a risky activity for children?

1.

2.

3.

4.

Q.53　According to the passage what may happen to a child who is never exposed to new risks?

1.

2.

3.

4.

Q.54　The main focus of this passage is...

1.

2.

3.

4.

 Section II

Q.55　Which of the following was not listed as a benefit of challenging new activities in the passage?

1.
2.
3.
4.

Listening Passage 2 Q.56- Q.60

Q.56　When should a child's homework routine be established?

1.
2.
3.
4.

Q.57　What is the best way to determine the location of your child's homework space?

1.
2.
3.
4.

Q.58　Which of the following is NOT offered as positive homework incentive?

1.
2.
3.
4.

 Section II

Q.59　Which of the following would the author be likely to NOT
　　　recommend?

1.

2.

3.

4.

Q.60　What is the best choice for a title for the passage?

1.

2.

3.

4.

Listening Passage 3 Q.61-Q.66 A Description of IB Curriculum Programs

Q.61　Which of the following year groups does IB support?

1.

2.

3.

4.

Q.62　According to the passage, how is the IB program radically
　　　different from traditional educational approaches?

1.

2.

3.

4.

Q.63　Where was the IB program founded?

1.

2.

3.

4.

 Section II

Q.64　Which of the following was not mentioned as a curriculum value of the IB Program?

1.

2.

3.

4.

Q.65　Based on the passage, do you feel the IB program is a quality approach to education?

1.

2.

3.

4.

Q.66　Which of the following is TRUE about the IB Program?

1.

2.

3.

4.

Pre- 1

第2回　問題

時間	筆記（英作文含む）　50分	リスニング　30分	
問題数	筆記　40問　英作文　1問	リスニング　25問	
点数	筆記　1問1点　英作文　10点	リスング　1問2点	
解答	筆記、リスニング	解答用紙（マークシート）	
	英作文	英作文専用用紙	

注意事項　　　この問題の複製（コピー）転用を禁じます。

Section I

A word or phrase is missing in each of the sentences. Select the best answer to complete the sentence. Mark the number 1, 2, 3 or 4 on your answer sheet. (Please fill in the entire circle darkly and completely.)

Q.1　　(　) did Taro enjoy the party, but also he made lots of new friends there as well.

1. Definitely　　　2. Not only　　　3. Somewhat　　　4. Consequently

Q.2　　Rie should really (　) these old smelly inside shoes.

1. get free of　　　2. get free from　　　3. ridden　　　4. get rid of

Q.3　　At Kid Patio we hold regular emergency response training (　) the year.

1. between　　　2. into　　　3. throughout　　　4. around

Q.4　　Since the BBQ is all you can eat, feel free to (　) if you are still hungry.

1. ask for alternatives
2. repeat the meal
3. ask for seconds
4. ask for duplicates

Q.5　　It looks like we'll be having a heavy downpour this morning, let's (　) the umbrella holder for everyone.

1. put out　　　2. put up　　　3. put in　　　4. put on

Q.6　　My wife's health still isn't (　) yet, so she can't leave the hospital.

1. vulnerable　　　2. calm　　　3. imbalanced　　　4. stable

　　　無断転載・複写を禁じます

Section I

Q.7　　The (　　) for my baby is in September, so I probably need to go on leave from the end of August.

　　　1. birthing day
　　　2. due date
　　　3. commencement date
　　　4. birth certificate

Q.8　　Eri seems to be really (　　) loud noises. She always covers her ears and screams.

　　　1. consumed by　　　2. belittled by　　　3. taken by　　　4. bothered by

---

Q.9-Q.10　Choose the best answer from the choices below the question.

Q.9　　What does the expression "much better than it used to be" mean?

　　　1. That something has improved.
　　　2. It is used to describe an increase in skill.
　　　3. That something used to be better.
　　　4. That the value of an item has changed.

Q.10　　What does it mean to "persevere"?

　　　1. To become drastically more ill.
　　　2. To continue an action when facing challenges.
　　　3. To transfer strategies after careful consideration.
　　　4. To sweat profusely during strenuous exercise.

Section II

Dialogues-A word or phrase is missing in each of the sentences. Select the best answer to complete the sentence. Mark the number 1, 2, 3 or 4 on your answer sheet. (Please fill in the entire circle darkly and completely.)

Dialogue 1 Q.11-Q.15　　　　　Conversation between two parents, Mariko and Judy

Mariko:　Hey Judy, welcome back! We missed you! Is that the new baby?

Judy:　Thank you! Yup this is our naughty little James. He's a (Q.11).

Mariko:　I bet! You must be so much more (Q.12) now though. Since he's your second child.

Judy:　Yeah, we were a bit (Q.13) with our first, but it's much easier now with the experience.

Mariko:　That's great to hear! How is his eating coming along?

Judy:　Step by step. He is still breastfeeding now, but I am planning to (Q.14) solid foods in about a month.

Mariko:　I bet you can't wait for that. (Q.15) a baby can really sap all your energy.

Judy:　Tell me about it! I am counting down the day!

Mariko:　Exactly! Still lots of practice time to go. Let's cross our fingers!

Q.11　　1. spoonful　　　2. mouthful　　　3. armful　　　4. handful

Q.12　　1. worried　　　2. belabored　　　3. relaxed　　　4. tense

Q.13　　1. casual　　　2. stressed　　　3. intolerant　　　4. free

Q.14　　1. introduce　　　2. conclude　　　3. finish　　　4. beginning

Q.15　　1. Milking　　　2. Nursing　　　3. Pasteurizing　　　4. Doctoring

 Section II

Dialogue 2 Q.16-Q.20   Phone conversation between a parent and the preschool director

Parent: We really love your school and I think we would like to (Q.16) our son immediately.

Director: I am really delighted to hear that. Please just allow me a moment to (Q.17) the school registry to ensure we have an open space available.

Parent: Thank you so much! I really hope you there is an availability.

Director: It seems there is! Can you tell me a bit about your child's (Q.18)?

Parent: Well she began speaking at 18 months, and has been eating solid food for a year. Though she (Q.19) will need help with her button, because her fine motor skills aren't quite there yet.

Director: Okay, no problem. Now all you have to do is provide us a copy of her health insurance and pay the initial enrollment fees. We then can consider the application (Q.20) concluded.

Q.16   1. application   2. transfer   3. enroll   4. terminate

Q.17   1. establish   2. double check   3. corroborate   4. authenticate

Q.18   1. enlargement   2. maturity   3. development   4. evolution

Q.19   1. high probability   2. uncertainly   3. most likely   4. most probably

Q.20   1. process   2. practice   3. proceeding   4. operation

Section III

In this section of the test you will read 2 passages. The first passage is followed by 15 questions related to information or vocabulary in the reading passage. The second passage is followed by 10 questions. Please choose the best answer for each question.

Reading Passage 1 Q.21-Q.35

The Power of Outdoor Classroom as a Catalyst for Creativity

When you think of creativity what comes to mind? For most of us it is the arts: drawing, painting, writing, or dancing. While those are indisputably creative (Q.21), creativity is also a way of thinking and learning across all (Q.22). Being creative is about making (Q.23) and seeing things from different (Q.24). It includes problem-solving, flexible thinking, and strategizing.

(Q.25), perhaps now more than ever, we need people who can use creativity to solve problems, adapt to a variety of situations, and communicate effectively with others. We need people who are critical thinkers, on the lookout for better ways of doing things and "doers", ready to express their creativity (Q.26) ideas.

Our ability to think creatively, as with other skills, grows with nurturing and use. (Q.27) provide opportunities for children to work creatively? Regular time outdoors in nature is one time-tested way to fuel creativity. Nature effectively invites the hands-on, messy play that nourishes children's creative problem-solving while also providing encounters with real challenges to remedy. Natural outdoor classrooms are creative laboratories for children to learn effectively in ways that (Q.28) human evolution and the latest brain research.

Evolutionary science tells us that the brain is designed to solve problems. Brain research shows that the mind operates most effectively when the body is in motion. The brain is not designed to sit still and memorize. The evidence is indisputable: aerobic exercise physically remodels our brains for peak performance. (Q.29) our brains are concerned, if we aren't moving, there is no real need to learn anything. So, if movement is (Q.30) to learning, how do traditional educational environments (indoor classrooms) ideally supporting learning? Some experts believe if you wanted to create an educational environment that was directly opposed to what the brain was good at doing, you probably would design something like a classroom.

Conversely, well-designed and nature-filled outdoor classrooms that encourage children's movement and that are ripe with opportunities for making choices, truly support flexible and creative thinking. Natural outdoor classrooms provide for strong brain development. They are ideal places for play and learning. These spaces afford young children many opportunities for investigation, problem-solving, thinking, rethinking, and refining their notions and understanding of how the world works.

Section III

The adult role outdoors in supporting creativity should not be underestimated. Creativity flourishes (Q.34) regular outdoor time for children and their important role in supporting student learning. Adults make important decisions in-the-moment as they decide when to jump in to assist with challenging tasks, when to join as a play partner, when to encourage children to take the lead, and when being an observer is what is most supportive.

Q.21-Q.24 Please choose from the following words to fit the blanks for Q.21-Q.24 in the first paragraph. Choose from the list below.

1. connections   2. perspectives   3. endeavors   4. domains

Q.25-Q.29 Please choose from following phrases to fit the blanks for Q.25 -Q.29 in the second paragraph. Choose from the list below.

Q.25   1. As a scholar   2. With hope   3. As a society   4. With some reluctance

Q.26   1. role-playing out   2. by trying out   3. auditioning with   4. by appraising some

Q.27   1. When we   2. If we   3. Who can   4. How can we

Q.28   1. congruent with
           2. mysteriously elongate
           3. counter intuitive to
           4. are compatible with

Q.29   1. In so many words   2. As long as   3. As far as   4. If and when

Q.30   Choose from the list of words below that best fits the blank.

1. essential   2. optional   3. auxiliary   4. inferior

Section III

Q.31 According to paragraphs 4 and 5, which of the following is NOT true about learning?

1. Traditional classrooms are not good for learning.

2. Outdoor classrooms allow opportunities for problem solving.

3. Movement should be minimized to reduce student distractions.

4. Outdoor classrooms make sense according to brain research.

Q.32 What does the phrase" time-tested" mean, as it is used in paragraph 3?

1. Something that is based on scientific research.

2. Something that has been proven true over a long period.

3. Something that has been carefully calculated.

4. Something that still needs time to verify.

Q.33 Which of the following is a synonym for 'underestimated' as it is used in paragraph 6?

1. commended   2. forgotten   3. lauded   4. undervalued

Q.34 What is the correct order of the words deleted from paragraph 6 ?
(＊答えの選択肢の文頭は小文字で記載しています)

1 the   2 understand   3 educators   4 value
5 when   6 of

1. 5-3-2-1-4-6   3. 6-1-2-4-5-3
2. 2-3-1-4-5-6   4. 3-5-1-4-2-6

Section III

Q.35　According to the passage, what is a benefit of motion?

1. It helps to reduce student stress.

2. It helps to burn excess energy and increases focus.

3. It helps the mind to operate more effectively.

4. It's fun and relaxing, and is a nice break from study.

Reading Passage 2 Q.36 -Q.40

A Letter from Kids Patio Preschool Regarding the Family Picnic

Dear Kids Patio Families,

Fall is nearly upon us and we are excited to (Q.36) the date for our Family Picnic. The annual Kids Patio Family Picnic will be held on Friday, October 20th from 1:00pm-4:00pm and will be a full event. All Kids Patio Families from both our Hiroo and Meguro campuses are welcome to join us for this special family event. This campus joining event will be held at Meguro Koen, which is located (Q.37) across the street from our Meguro campus. TIK will be offering a free bus service to and from the event location for all of our Hiroo families.

The Kid Patio Family Picnic will be a potluck style picnic where families can enjoy the beautiful scenery at the park while enjoying a (Q.38) lunch. TIK children will be engaged with games and activities throughout the picnic and will have a chance to participate in a treasure hunt. This will be a sports day style event, where children and parents will join together to perform various sporting activities. Parents please come dressed appropriately for active participation in these fun activities with your children.

For the potluck picnic portion of the event we ask that each family bring some type of snack or food dish to contribute to the picnic. Each family should bring enough food to feed 10-20 people. Paper plates, cups, forks, knives, chopsticks, and drinks will be provided by Kids Patio. Please keep in mind that any food products containing nuts or raw egg are not allowed as we have children with allergy

 Section III

restrictions. We also ask that each family bring a park blanket for their family to sit on during the picnic. Furthermore, we are accepting candy donations for our Treasure Hunt. If you would like to contribute some treats for the hunt, then please drop them off at one of our school offices.

All families are to meet at Kids Patio Meguro at 12:40 on the day of the event. We will leave Kids Patio Meguro to head over to Meguro Koen at 12:50pm. Afternoon program children and their families are also asked to arrive at Kids Patio Meguro at 12:40. Any families that are not able to arrive by 12:40 will simply be asked to meet us later at the park. A park map will be disseminated at a later date.

In the event of rain, the event will be rescheduled for Friday, October 27th from 1:00pm-4:00pm. If both dates are rained out, the event will regrettably be cancelled as we understand it is not easy for our families to make changes to their personal and work schedules. With that in mind, we are hoping to have some beautiful weather and are looking forward to another wonderful event!

Sincerely,
Principal Yamada

For Q.36-Q.38

Choose a word from the list below that best fits in the blank spaces in the sentences marked (Q.36), (Q.37) and (Q.38). One choice does not fit any of the blank spaces.

1. leisurely　　　　2. announce　　　　3. observe　　　　4. directly

 Section III

Q.39   According to the letter, what will happen in the event of rain?

1. The event will continue regardless of weather.

2. The event will be postponed one hour.

3. The event will be cancelled.

4. The event will be rescheduled only once.

Q.40   According to the letter, which of the following will was NOT mentioned as an event activity?

1. Sporting activities

2. Group singing

3. A treasure hunt

4. Various games

 Section IV

Writing

Q.41 Composition

Ms. Suzuki:　　Where are you headed for Summer vacation this year?

Ms. Yamanaka: I leave this Saturday for Honolulu. I am so excited!

Ms. Suzuki:　　Wow, sounds exotic! What are your plans in Honolulu?

Ms. Yamanaka: I am actually going to take some surfing lessons. I've always wanted to learn.

Ms. Suzuki:　　I actually know a great surf instructor on Waikiki Beach. Let me give you his contact info.

Ms. Yamanaka: Wow, that would be great!

Q.41　　　In this section you will read a dialog. In 30-35 words, write a summary of the dialog you just read.

Evaluation points:

①Your answer will be evaluated for the correct use of grammar and sentence structure, proper spelling and punctuation. (Commas, periods and other punctuations are not included in the number of words.)

②Your answer will be evaluated by how effectively and efficiently you communicate the information in the dialog.

第2回　問題
Listening Test

準1級リスニングテストについて
（テスト開始までの一分間で下記をよく読んでください）

●このテストはSection IとSection IIにわかれています。
●放送の間、メモをとっても構いません。
●最後のQ.66の後、10秒するとテスト終了の合図がありますので、筆記用具を置いて答えの記入をやめてください。

Section I (Q.42-Q.50)	イラストを参考にしながら、対話を聞き、その質問に対して最も適切な答えを1,2,3,4の中から一つ選ぶ形式です。 対話と質問は、1回ずつ放送されます。
Section II (Q.51-Q.66)	英文を聞き、最も適切な答えを1,2,3,4の中から一つ選ぶ形式です。 英文と答えは、1回ずつ放送されます。

Section I

In this section of the test you will hear four dialogues. After each dialogue there are some questions. Choose the best answer from the list below the questions.

Dialogue 1 Q.42-Q.46

Q.42　What did Ms. Yamanaka do to make Principal Yamada disappointed?

1.

2.

3.

4.

Q.43　According to Principal Yamada, what should have Ms. Yamanaka done about her situation?

1.

2.

3.

4.

Q.44　How does Ms. Yamanaka feel about her first year teaching?

1.

2.

3.

4.

Q.45　What is Ms. Yamanaka going to do to make the situation better?

1.

2.

3.

4.

 Section I

Q.46　What will happen if Ms. Yamanaka doesn't respect her boss in the future?
1.
2.
3.
4.

Dialogue 2 Q.47-Q.51

Q.47　Why is Ms. Ishikawa thankful to Principal Yamada?
1.
2.
3.
4.

Q.48　What does Ms. Ishikawa discuss with Principal Yamada?
1.
2.
3.
4.

Q.49　What is a good point about many international schools?
1.
2.
3.
4.

Q.50　Why does Ms. Ishikawa feel sad for Ayaka?
1.
2.
3.
4.

 Section II

Listening Passage 1 Q.51-Q.55　　Removing the Bubble Wrap

Q.51　What could happen if parents do not allow their children to experience new sensations?

1.

2.

3.

4.

Q.52　Why should children be allowed to play in high places?

1.

2.

3.

4.

Q.53　What risk is NOT given as a way to boost confidence?

1.

2.

3.

4.

Q.54　What does risky play help children overcome?

1.

2.

3.

4.

Q.55　Why is the title of this passage "Removing the Bubble Wrap"?

1.

2.

3.

4.

 Section II

Listening Passage 2 Q.56-Q.60

Q.56　What is NOT one of the things mentioned that distracts children from homework?

1.

2.

3.

4.

Q .57　According to the speaker, what should parents do on the first day of school?

1.

2.

3.

4.

Q.58　Where is a good place for children to study at home?

1.

2.

3.

4.

Q.59　Why is it a good idea to do homework after dinner?

1.

2.

3.

4.

Q.60　What would be the best title for this passage?

1.

2.

3.

4.

 Section II

Listening Passage 3 Q.61-Q.66

Q.61　What age levels does the IB Program provide services for?
1.
2.
3.
4.

Q.62　What does the IB organization check when visiting a school?
1.
2.
3.
4.

Q.63　How are students graded under the IB Program?
1.
2.
3.
4.

Q.64　What was the IB curriculum designed to accomplish?
1.
2.
3.
4.

Q.65　What do the students create during the year?
1.
2.
3.
4.

 Section II

Q.66　　What is the benefit of graduating from the IB Program?

1.

2.

3.

4.

Pre-
1

第3回　問題

時間	筆記（英作文含む）　50分	リスニング　30分
問題数	筆記　40問　英作文　1問	リスニング　25問
点数	筆記　1問1点　英作文　10点	リスング　1問2点
解答	筆記、リスニング	解答用紙（マークシート）
	英作文	英作文専用用紙

注意事項　　　この問題の複製（コピー）転用を禁じます。

Section I

A word or phrase is missing in each of the sentences. Select the best answer to complete the sentence. Mark the number 1, 2, 3 or 4 on your answer sheet. (Please fill in the entire circle darkly and completely.)

Q.1　Taro threw up (　) three times this morning.

1. a sum of　　　2. a quotient of　　　3. a portion　　　4. a total of

Q.2　Rie did you (　) for ballet classes yet?

1. agreement　　　2. sign up　　　3. confirmation　　　4. reservation

Q.3　Everyone please (　) your seat belts for safety!

1. buckle　　　2. mend　　　3. unhook　　　4. disengage

Q.4　I am a bit (　) about Taro's health. He hasn't eaten in days.

1. encouraged　　　2. concerned　　　3. surprised　　　4. supportive

Q.5　There was very heavy rains last night and all the roads are (　).

1.misty　　　2. blizzard　　　3.humidity　　　4. flooded

Q.6　Taro is being (　) this morning and won't get dressed.

1. appreciative　　　2. easy　　　3. difficult　　　4. imbalanced

Q.7　If you make a wish maybe someday it will (　).

1. come true　　　2. due true　　　3. arrive true　　　4. go true

 Section I

Q.8　　　I'm (　　) Taro won't make it to the party because he is ill.

　　　　1. put on　　　　　2. afraid that　　　　3. consumed with　　　4. bothered by

Q.9-Q.10 Choose the best answer from the choices below the question.

Q.9　　　What does the expression "first come first serve" mean?

　　　　1. that people who arrive early must help assist others
　　　　2. that arriving early improves your performance
　　　　3. that everyone must arrive in the order they are scheduled
　　　　4. that people are served in the order that they arrive

Q.10　　What does it mean to be "keen"?

　　　　1. to be sly
　　　　2. to like something or be interested in doing it
　　　　3. to be intelligent and charming
　　　　4. to oppose an activity or suggestion

Section II

Dialogues-A word or phrase is missing in each of the sentences. Select the best answer to complete the sentence. Mark the number 1,2,3 or 4 on your answer sheet. (Please fill in the entire circle darkly and completely.)

Dialogue 1 Q.11-Q.15   Conversation between two parents, Mariko and Judy

Mariko: Hey Judy! Did you receive the Sports Day (Q.11)?

Judy: Yes, the schedule of (Q.12) this year looks absolutely amazing!

Mariko: Kotone is super excited about the tug-of war!

Judy: Hey do you know if parents are able to (Q.13) with their children?

Mariko: Yup! Families can join together in pretty much everything.

Judy: Wow! That is (Q.14) fantastic news!

Mariko: Do you know what the weather is going to be like on that day?

Judy: At the moment the weather report says hot and sunny.

Mariko: Okay, I will make sure to (Q.15) lots of sunscreen for the kids.

Q.11   1. cancellation   2. program   3. manifest   4. diagram

Q.12   1. happenings   2. postponements   3. tasks   4. events

Q.13   1. qualify   2. participate   3. separate   4. forfeit

Q.14   1. absolutely   2. partially   3. dubiously   4. questionably

Q.15   1. pack   2. bundle   3. compact   4. bunch

Section II

Dialogue 2 Q.16-Q.20　　　　Phone conversation between a parent and the preschool director

Parent:　　Hello! I was wondering if you could help to support us for the children's (Q.16) at our end of year concert?

Director:　Absolutely! I would be more than happy to (Q.17)

Parent:　　Thank you so much! Do you think you could help to coordinate the children's (Q.18)? They each must dress as a different animal.

Director:　Sure! I will make sure to have all the costumes done (Q.19) to the rehearsal.

Parent:　　Thank you! It would be so wonderful to have them ready before we officially start practice.

Director:　You can (Q.20) on me! I'll get started straight away.

Q.16　　1. achievement　　2. performance　　3. exam　　4. enrollment

Q.17　　1. help with　　2.help in　　3. help on　　4. help out

Q.18　　1. costumes　　2. uniforms　　3. equipment　　4. apparel

Q.19　　1. after　　2. prior　　3. following　　4. subsequent

Q.20　　1. believe　　2. count　　3. trust　　4. plan

Section III

In this section of the test you will read 2 passages. The first passage is followed by 15 questions related to information or vocabulary in the reading passage. The second passage is followed by 10 questions. Please choose the best answer for each question. (Please fill in the entire circle darkly and completely.)

Reading Passage 1 Q.21-Q.35

Reading Passage 1 Q.21-Q.35

Early Childhood Education is the Key to Life-Long Success

"The sooner the better" is the (Q.21) slogan for early childhood education. There is no magic bullet to ensure a (Q.22) of self-fulfillment in personal and career terms, but rigorous (Q.23) shows that high-quality early childhood education is an extraordinarily powerful means to (Q.24) continued success in school, the workplace, and also in social realms.

(Q.25) surprising, but the experiences of children in their early years have a much larger impact (Q.26) to experiences during their school years and beyond. If children lag in those early years, chances are that they will never (Q.27). Trying to strengthen areas of weakness in learning is much more difficult and expensive than learning early on. The good news is that high-quality programs (Q.28) early childhood years can have powerful long-term impacts for children of all backgrounds.

A recent study (Q.29) children who attend high-quality preschools are not only more likely to graduate from high school and college, but they are more likely to earn more money once they start their careers. These children when adults are also more likely to become parents and own a home, and are less likely to have drug or substance (Q.30) problems. Long-term studies also show that these children are less likely to be arrested for crimes in the future.

This research shows that if all adults have a kick-start through high-quality early childhood education, our entire society benefits. Fewer people will need government welfare support, crime rates will decrease, and our population as a whole will be healthier. Society will also benefit from a much more skilled workforce.

High-quality early childhood education is not **a magic bullet** to ensure that those participating will be destined to be successful in and out of school for the rest of their lives. Lots of other factors have real impact, but the evidence is **overwhelming** that the social and economic benefits of high-quality early education for children are both substantial and lasting. (Q.34) who participate, but also our society as a whole.

 Section III

Q.21-Q.24 Please choose from the following words to fit the blanks for Q.21 -Q.24 in the first paragraph. Choose from the list below.

1. research   2. perfect   3. lifetime   4. promote

Q.25-Q.29 Please choose from following phrases to fit the blanks for Q.25 -Q.29 in the second paragraph.
Choose from the list below.

Q.25   1. It may become   3. It doesn't
        2. Some might say   4. It may seem

Q.26   1. in comparison   3. in hindsight
        2. in retrospect   4. in correlation

Q.27   1. reach up   3. catch up
        2. catch on   4. reach on

Q.28   1. converged on   3. focused on
        2. divided amongst   4. dispersed from

Q.29   1. showed that   3. displayed that
        2. concealed that   4. withheld that

Q.30 -Q.35 Please choose the answer that best fits the question

Q.30   Choose from the list of words below that best fits the blank.

1. obedience   2. preservation   3. desecration   4. abuse

Section III

Q.31　According to paragraphs 3 and 4, which of the following is NOT a benefit of high-quality early childhood education?

1. Lower crime rates.
2. A healthier population.
3. Decreased rates of mental retardation.
4. Less people on welfare.

Q.32　What does the phrase **magic bullet** mean, as it is used in paragraph 5?

1. A sensible plan.
2. Requirement.
3. A plan left to random chance.
4. A fool proof solution.

Q.33　Which of the following is a synonym for **overwhelming** as it is used in paragraph 5?

1. staggering　　　　2. inadequate　　　　3. lacking　　　　4. meager

Q.34　What is the correct order of the words deleted from paragraph 5?
（*答えの選択肢の文頭は小文字で記載しています）

1 benefits　　　　2 not　　　　　3 children　　　　4 just
5 the　　　　　　6 this

1.　5-3-2-1-4-6　　　　3.　6-1-2-4-5-3
2.　2-3-1-4-5-6　　　　4.　3-5-1-4-2-6

 Section III

Q.35   According to the passage, high-quality early education primarily benefits (　　)?

1. low-income children.

2. wealth children.

3. children from minority backgrounds.

4. all children.

 Section III

Reading Passage 2 Q.36 -Q.40

A Letter from Kids Patio Preschool Regarding the Summer Charity Project

Dear Kids Patio Families,

We are excited to announce that we will be hosting a Summer Charity Event again this year. Last year's project with the Red Cross Foundation was so (Q.36), that we decided to do another event this year. This year we will be holding a sponsored "Mini-Marathon". Each child will receive a sponsor sheet and will go out to find sponsors who will donate money to them to participate in and finish their charity race. The length of the race will be as follows:

For children under 3.5 years old – 500 meters

For children above 3.5 years old – 1,000 meters

This event will take place during the normal school day and will not be open to parents. The reason being is that it is rainy season, and the scheduling must remain tentative and (Q.37). For this event we will be working with the 4Ocean charity, which helps to remove plastic and waste from world's oceans and shorelines. This is an incredibly valuable initiative as it will to not only save countless numbers of marine wildlife, but it will also help to (Q.38) the beauty of our planet.

Sponsor forms will be going home in your child's backpacks today. Please discuss this important initiative with them and return all sponsorships and donations in an envelope with your child's full name by Friday, June 8th. If you have any questions please communicate with your child's classroom teacher. Thank you for your support!

Sincerely,
Principal Yamada

 Section III

Q.36-Q.38 Choose a word from the list below that best fits in the blank spaces in the sentences marked (Q.36), (Q.37) and (Q.38). One choice does not fit any of the blank spaces.

1. flexible   2. preserve   3. successful   4. collaborate

Q.39   According to the letter, when should parents arrive for the event?

1. On Friday, June 8th.
2. Only after their child has found a sponsor.
3. After the rainy season.
4. Parents are not allowed to attend.

Q.40   According to the letter, which of the following is NOT a benefit of the charity event?

1. Saving marine wildlife
2. Removing trash from the ocean
3. Taking a trip to the beach
4. Protecting the beauty of our planet

 Section IV

Writing

Ms. Suzuki:　　What did you do this weekend, Ms. Yamanaka?

Ms. Yamanaka: I went to Disney Land with my boyfriend on Saturday morning!

Ms. Suzuki:　　Wow, that sounds exciting. How was it?

Ms. Yamanaka: Well we got there at 8am just when it opened, so we were able to ride so many rides!

Ms. Suzuki:　　That's great. My favorite ride is Splash Mountain.

Ms. Yamanaka: Me too⋯but sadly it was closed for repairs. It will re-open next month.

Q.41　　　In this section you will read a dialog. In 30-35 words, write a summary of the dialog you just read.

Evaluation points:

　　　①Your answer will be evaluated for the correct use of grammar and sentence structure, proper spelling and punctuation. (Commas, periods and other punctuations are not included in the number of words.)

　　　②Your answer will be evaluated by how effectively and efficiently you communicate the information in the dialog.

第3回　問題
Listening Test

準1級リスニングテストについて
（テスト開始までの一分間で下記をよく読んでください）

●このテストはSection ⅠとSection Ⅱにわかれています。
●放送の間、メモをとっても構いません。
●最後のQ.66の後、10秒するとテスト終了の合図がありますので、筆記用具を置いて答えの記入をやめてください。

Section Ⅰ (Q.42-Q.50)　　　イラストを参考にしながら、対話を聞き、その質問に対して最も適切な答えを1,2,3,4の中 から一つ選ぶ形式です。対話と質問は、 1回ずつ放送されます。。

Section Ⅱ (Q.51-Q.66)　　　英文を聞き、最も適切な答えを1,2,3,4の中から一つ選ぶ形式です。英文と答えは、1回ずつ放送されます。

Section I

Dialogue 1 Q.42-Q.46

Q.42　Why did Principal Yamada want to meet with Ms. Yamaguchi?

1.

2.

3.

4.

Q.43　What was Principal Yamada's main issue with Ms. Yamaguchi?

1.

2.

3.

4.

Q.44　What was Ms. Yamaguchi's first excuse for her behavior?

1.

2.

3.

4.

Q.45　Why do you think Ms. Yamaguchi is struggling with her role?

1.

2.

3.

4.

Section I

Q.46　What will happen if Ms. Yamaguchi's poor performance continues?

1.

2.

3.

4.

Dialogue 2 Q.47-Q.51

Q.47　It's clear from the passage that the meeting was...

1.

2.

3.

4.

Q.48　What is Ms. Iwamoto's issue?

1.

2.

3.

4.

Q.49　It is clear from the passage that the problem teacher...

1.

2.

3.

4.

Q.50　What was Mrs. Iwamoto's final decision?

1.

2.

3.

4.

 Section II

Listening Passage 1 Q.51-Q.55

Q.51　How often is Open House held?
1.
2.
3.
4.

Q.52　Which of the following WON'T parents be able to do at Open House?
1.
2.
3.
4.

Q.53　What does the letter NOT warn about children's behavior?
1.
2.
3.
4.

Q.54　What will happen in the event of a late signup for Open House?
1.
2.
3.
4.

 Section II

Q.55   From the letter, what do you feel is the main purpose of
        Open House?

1.

2.

3.

4.

Listening Passage 2 Q.56-Q.60

Q.56   What will the school do in response to the problem?

1.

2.

3.

4.

Q .57   How many cases of Hand Foot and Mouth Disease are
        currently at Kids Patio?

1.

2.

3.

4.

Q.58.   Which of the following is NOT a symptom of the disease?

1.

2.

3.

4.

 Section II

Q.59　According to the letter, why are Kids Patio students particularly at risk for the disease?

1.

2.

3.

4.

Q.60　According to the letter how long should infected children be kept out of school?

1.

2.

3.

4.

Listening Passage 3 Q.61-Q.66

Q.61　Why is differentiation important in the classroom?

1.

2.

3.

4.

Q.62　What do you think the author means by the term "scaling lesson content"?

1.

2.

3.

4.

Section II

Q.63　What is the ideal way to host a reading lesson?

1.

2.

3.

4.

Q.64　What does the passage note as a benefit of differentiated homework?

1.

2.

3.

4.

Q.65　Which of the following was not mentioned in the passage as a differentiation strategy?

1.

2.

3.

4.

Q.66　Based on what you learned from the passage,what is a likely consequence of not differentiating in the classroom?

1.

2.

3.

4.

解答解説

第1回　問題

解答解説

Level Pre-1 第1回　解答

Q.1	3
Q.2	2
Q.3	4
Q.4	1
Q.5	3
Q.6	3
Q.7	4
Q.8	2
Q.9	1
Q.10	2
Q.11	4
Q.12	2
Q.13	3
Q.14	1
Q.15	2
Q.16	4
Q.17	3
Q.18	3
Q.19	2
Q.20	1

Q.21	2
Q.22	4
Q.23	1
Q.24	3
Q.25	3
Q.26	2
Q.27	2
Q.28	1
Q.29	4
Q.30	4
Q.31	2
Q.32	3
Q.33	3
Q.34	4
Q.35	1
Q.36	2
Q.37	3
Q.38	1
Q.39	4
Q.40	2

Q.42	1
Q.43	3
Q.44	3
Q.45	2
Q.46	4
Q.47	2
Q.48	3
Q.49	4
Q.50	1
Q.51	4
Q.52	2
Q.53	3
Q.54	3
Q.55	2
Q.56	4
Q.57	2
Q.58	1
Q.59	4
Q.60	2
Q.61	4
Q62	3
Q.63	4
Q.64	1
Q.65	1
Q.66	2

Q.41

Ms. Suzuki is wondering if Ms. Yamanaka will attend the BBQ on Sunday, but Ms. Yamanaka has a doctor's appointment. Ms. Suzuki suggests if she brings wine, she can arrive late to the BBQ.(30 words)

Section I

Q.1　正解　　3　　　　Currently

解説　[現在、私たちの保育園には 25 人の子ども達が入園しています。先生 1 人に対し、園児 5 人の割合です] という内容ですから、3.[Currently(現在)] が正解です。1.[Forthwith]、2.[Straightaway]、4.[Momentarily] いずれも、[すぐに] という意味です。

Q.2　正解　　2　　　　buckle

解説　[いいですか、みなさん、水族館に出かける準備ができましたよ。出発する前に座席ベルトをしめてくださいね] という内容ですから、2.[buckle(締め金で留める)] が正解です。1.[clasp] は [留め金]、3.[harness] は [(馬に) 装具をつける]、4.[clip] は「(はさみなどで) 切る] の意味です。

Q.3　正解　　4　　　　bumper to bumper

解説　[遅くなってしまいごめんなさい。今朝は大渋滞でした] という内容ですから、4.[bumper to bumper(数珠繋ぎの、渋滞の)] が正解です。1.[toe to toe] は [向かいあって (戦う)]、3.[back to back] は [背中合わせで] という意味です。2.[neck to neck] は存在しません。

Q.4　正解　　1　　　　misty

解説　[外は、まだ雨が降っていますか？そうでもないですけど、ちょっと霧がかかっています] という内容ですから、1.[misty(霧のかかった)] が正解です。2.[humidity] は [湿気、湿度]、3.[hail] は [あられ、ひょう]、4.[downpour] は [どしゃぶり、豪雨] という意味です。

Q.5　正解　　3　　　　wear hats and gloves

解説　[明日は大雪になりそうですから、子ども達は登校時、帽子と手袋を着用してきてもらいます] という内容ですから、3.[wear hats and gloves(帽子と手袋を身に付ける)] が正解です。

Q.6　正解　　3　　　　come true

解説　[ろうそくを吹き消したら自分の願い事は自分の中にしまっておいてね、そうしないと叶わないかもしれないから] という内容ですから、3.[come true(叶う)] が正解です。

 Section I

Q.7　　正解　　4　　　　　Participation

　　　解説　　[明日の夜、保護者の会を開きます。保護者全員の方の参加が必要となっています
　　　　　　　ので、ご参加ください。それでは、明晩お待ちしています] という内容ですから、
　　　　　　　4 .[Participation(参加)] が正解です。

Q.8　　正解　　2　　　　　cast

　　　解説　　[今年の園の劇の配役が選ばれました。みんな、上手な役者さんですよ] という内
　　　　　　　容ですから、2.[cast(役者、出演者)] が正解です。1.[roster] は [名簿]、3.[attendance]
　　　　　　　は [出席] です。

Q.9　　What does the expression "it slipped my mind" mean?
　　　　"it slipped my mind" という表現の意味は何ですか？

　　　1.　　　　to have forgotten something

　　　2.　　　　to have become confused

　　　3.　　　　to have not understood

　　　4.　　　　to become nervous

　　　正解　　1　　　　　to have forgotten something

　　　解説　　[Slip someone's mind] は「うっかり忘れる」「度忘れする」「つい忘れる」という
　　　　　　　意味なので、1.[to have forgotten something(何か忘れてしまった)] が正解です。

Q.10　　What does it mean when we say an illness is "going around"？ "going around" とはどのよう
　　　　な意味ですか？

　　　1.　　　　That the illness isn't particularly contagious.

　　　2.　　　　That many people have been catching the illness.

　　　3.　　　　The illness mostly affects travelers.

　　　4.　　　　The illness cannot be stopped by preventative medicine.

　　　正解　　2　　　　　That many people have been catching the illness.

　　　解説　　[go around] は、[（病気などが）広まる」という意味なので、2.[That many people
　　　　　　　have been catching the illness(多くの人が病気にかかっている)] が正解です。

 Section II

Dialogue 1　Q.11-Q.15　　　　保護者（マリコさんとジュディさん）二人の会話

Mariko:　ジュディさん、今年の子どもたちの劇は楽しみ？

Judy:　楽しみにしているのだけど、コナーの衣装を作るのがちょっと心配。彼は鳥を演じるの。

Mariko:　あら、良かったら、手伝うわよ。もうこういうのは、何年も作ってきているから。

Judy:　まぁ！それは、うれしいわ。申し出てくれてありがとう。とても助かるわ。

Mariko:　ぜんぜん問題ないわよ。私の方は、モモカのセリフが心配なのよ。覚えなければならないセリフがたくさんあるのよ。

Judy:　よくわかるわ。コナーもセリフをしゃべる時はドキドキしていたわ。

Mariko:　そうね、子ども達には結構大変よね。でもそれが彼らのリーダーシップを育てるんじゃないかと感じているわ。

Judy:　そうね、その通りね。本番までに何回かリハーサルがあるので良かったけどね。

Mariko:　そうよ！まだたくさん練習の時間があるしね。うまくいくように祈りましょう！

Q.11　　正解　　4　　　costume
　　　　解説　　[costume] は [衣装] という意味で正解です。

Q.12　　正解　　2　　　help out
　　　　解説　　[help out] は [困ったときに人を助ける] という意味があり正解です。

Q.13　　正解　　3　　　volunteering
　　　　解説　　[volunteering] は [自発的に進んで申し出る、(人) に手助けを申し出る] という意味があり正解です。

Q.14　　正解　　1　　　lines
　　　　解説　　[lines] は [セリフ] という意味なので正解です。

Q.15　　正解　　2　　　rehearsals
　　　　解説　　[rehearsals] は [リハーサル（下稽古）] という意味があり正解です。

Section II

Dialogue 2 Q.16-Q.20　　　　　保護者と園長先生の電話の会話

保護者：　急なお願いにもかかわらずお会いいただきましてありがとうございます。

園長：　　かまいませんよ、何かご心配でも?先週の節分行事で何か問題があったことを聞いています。

保護者：　そうなのです、あのお祭り以来、子どもが眠ることが出来ないのです。オニ役の先生が大声をはり
　　　　　上げたので子どもがうなされるようになっているのです。

園長：　　そうですか。お子さんがそのようないやな経験をされたとはとても申し訳ございません。

保護者：　とんでもないことです、日本文化を教えていただき皆様の努力に感謝しています。ただ、子どもが
　　　　　園のことでいやな思いになっているのを見ているのがつらいのです。

園長：　　この件、先生たち全員と話をし、来年の行事のやり方を状況に応じて見直すことをお約束しますの
　　　　　で、どうぞご安心なさってください。

保護者：　ありがとうございます。それを聞いてホッとしました。

園長：　　それでは、明朝お会いしましょう。

Q.16　　正解　　4　　　　agreeing
　　　　解説　　4.[agreeing] は [同意する、応じる] という意味です。1.[complying] は [従う]、
　　　　　　　　2.[denying] は [否定する]、3.[resisting] は [抵抗する] という意味です。

Q.17　　正解　　3　　　　raised their voice
　　　　解説　　[声を荒げる、どなる] という意味の 3.[raised their voice] が正解です。

Q.18　　正解　　3　　　　stressed out about
　　　　解説　　3.[stressed out about] は [〜で悩む、イライラする] という意味です。1.[burnt
　　　　　　　　out] は [燃え尽きた]、2.[put out] は [消す]、4.[drop out] は [落ちる] という意
　　　　　　　　味です。

Q.19　　正解　　2　　　　accordingly
　　　　解説　　2.[accordingly] は [状況に応じて適切に] という意味です。1.[correspondingly] は [相
　　　　　　　　応に]、3.[fixability] は [定着性]、4.[unsuitably] は [不適当に] という意味です。

 Section II

Q.20　　正解　　1　　　　　relieved

　　　　解説　　1.[be relieved] で [ホッとする、安心する] という意味です。2.[distraught] は [取
　　　　　　　　り乱した]、3.[pacified 原形 pacify] は [なだめる]、4.[alleviated（原形 alleviate）]
　　　　　　　　は [（苦痛を）軽くする] という意味です。

 Section III

Reading Passage 1 Q.21-Q.35

共感力　：子どもたちに相手の立場に立って、他者と気持ちを分かち合う大切さを教える

　　　　共感力は不思議な特質の一つです。ほとんどの人がその力を求めるのですが、どのようにその力を発揮し、受け止めることができるかを理解している人は少ないのです。自己満足度が強調される世の中では、共感力への要求は高いのに対してそれが得られることはあまりありません。この事が他者への共感力を発揮することの意義を次世代に教える理由に他なりません。

　　　　多くの人は同情と共感する力を混同していますが、それぞれは全く異なった意味をもっています。共感力にはより深い意味があります。それは他人がどう感じているか知るだけでなくその人の感情を大切に思い尊重する力なのです。それは、他者に対し、優しさや尊厳、思いやりを持って接することなのです。

　　　　生まれつきやさしい心を持っている子どもがいる一方、多くの子どもたちは周囲の大人が共感力を発揮しお手本を示す必要があります。それは親の子どもたちへの関わり方から始まります。親が子どもたちが大切にしていることに関心を持ち、積極的に思いやりを持ってその子どもたちの感情に寄り添うことこそが共感力を発揮する術を教えることになるのです。

　　　　子どもたちは自分の感情的な欲求が満たされた時に、他人の感情的な欲求を如何に満たすかを学びます。これは自身の感情的欲求が満たされた時にのみ実現可能となります。空の水差しはコップを満たすことは出来ません。多くの親は感情的欲求や感情について話すことは難しいと感じています。しかし、大人はこの不快感を乗り越え、子どもたちと感情について他者がそれをどのように感じたかを話し合うことがとても大切です。具体的な感情をあげてみてください。（たとえば、嫉妬、怒り、愛など）そして、これらの感情は普通のことであることを教えてください。どのように感情に前向きに向き合うかを話し、他の人がそれらの感情を体験している場面を示してください。日常起きることに置き換えて教えること以上のものはありません。他者に影響を与えている状況を探して、それがその人たちにとってどのような意味を持つのか、彼らがどう感じているのか、子どもたちに話してください。例えば、猛スピードで通り過ぎる救急車を見たとき、その病人の家族がどのように感じているかについて話してみてください。

　　　　幼い子どもたちは特に、他人や何か他のもののフリをしたがります。このような楽しい時間を使って共感力を教えることもできます。子どもたちに他人の役を演じさせてください。それは本やテレビのキャラクターかもしれないし、最近すごい経験をした知人でもかまいません。一緒にお話を演じて、子どもたちに演技を中断させ、ひとつの場面でそのキャラクターが何を感じたのか想像させることもできます。その状況下で他者が経験したかもしれない感情に子どもたちは注目するようになるのです。また、子どもたちにその人物の感情を顔で表現するよう聞いてみてもよい

Section III

でしょう。

　　　　　思いやりという贈り物を与えているのです。共感力を理解し発揮するよう子どもたちを育てることで、他者に与えることの大切さを贈り物として与えているのです。自分自身の徳を追及することが重要視される世の中で、他者へ与えることのできる人はめったにいません。しかし、そのような人こそが人生から最大の満足を享受し、最も意義ある人生を送り、何よりもかけがえのない人間関係を楽しんでいるのです。子どもたちに共感力を教える事は彼らの将来にとってまた、彼らが住む社会にとっても価値ある投資です。

思いやりという贈り物を与えているのです。共感力を理解し発揮するよう子どもたちを育てることで、他者に与えることの大切さを贈り物として与えているのです。自分自身の徳を追及することが重要視される世の中で、他者へ与えることのできる人はめったにいません。しかし、そのような人こそが人生から最大の満足を享受し、最も意義ある人生を送り、何よりもかけがえのない人間関係を楽しんでいるのです。子どもたちに共感力を教える事は彼らの将来にとってまた、彼らが住む社会にとっても価値ある投資です。

Q.21-Q.24

正解　　Q.21　2 qualities　Q.22　4 emphasized　Q.23　1 generation　Q.24　3 treating

解説　　Q.21　2.[qualities] は [特質、性質] という意味です。Q.22　自己満足が [強調される] という意味なので 4.[emphasized] が正解です。Q.23　[次の世代に] という内容ですから 1.[generation] が正解です。Q.24　[人に接する、人を扱う] は 3.[treating] が正解です。

Q.25-Q.30

正解　　Q.25　3 in most cases　Q.26　2 it begins with　Q.27　2 This can only be done　Q.28　1 real life example　Q.29　4 might be feeling　Q.30　4 pretend

解説　　Q.25　前段文章の [生まれつき優しい心を持っている子どもがいる一方での [while] に対比した 3.[in most cases] が正解です。Q.26 the way につながる文章は 2.[it begins with(～から始まる)] です。Q.27 when 以降の文章が成立するのは 2.[This can only be done(～の時のみ実現可能)] です。Q.28　real life example「実例」を挙げることが一番を受ける文章は 1.[There is nothing like(他にはない)] です。Q.29「感情」についての文章であるから 4.[might be feeling(どう感じているか)] です。Q.30　[他人のふりをしたがる] で 4.[pretend] が正解です。

Section III

Q.31　　正解　　2　　　　Role-play is not an effective method.
　　　　解説　　[段落4, 5中で子どもの共感力教育で正しくないのはどれでしょう] という設問
　　　　　　　です。2.[Role-play is not an effective method(他人の役を演じることは効果的方
　　　　　　　法ではない)] の記載内容は文章中で効果的方法と述べられています。

Q.32　　正解　　3　　　　You cannot give what you do not have.
　　　　解説　　段落4の [An empty jug cannot fill a cup.(空の水差しはコップを満たせない。)]
　　　　　　　と同じ意味は 3. [You cannot give what you do not have. (持っていない物を与える
　　　　　　　事はできません。)] が正解です。

Q.33　　正解　　3　　　　important
　　　　解説　　段落 5.[significant(意義深い、重要な) の同義語は] の設問ですから 3.[important]
　　　　　　　が正解です。

Q.34　　正解　　4　　　　you're giving the gift of compassion
　　　　解説　　(4-3-5-1-4-2-6) [you're giving the gift of compassion （思いやりという贈り物を与え
　　　　　　　てい　　　　る）]が正解です。

Q.35　　正解　　1　　　　They will live more meaningful lives.
　　　　解説　　文中から [what is a benefit of children practicing empathy?(子どもたちが共感力を
　　　　　　　習慣的に身につけて得られるものは何ですか？)] という設問です。1. [They will
　　　　　　　live more meaningful lives. (より有意義な人生を送るでしょう)] が正解です。

 Section III

Reading Passage 2 Q.36-Q.40　　キッズ・パティオ園からのオープンハウスについてのお知らせ

キッズ・パティオ御家族の皆様、

　　　　皆様お変わりはございませんか。オープンハウス参加申込み開始のお知らせです。オープンハウスは5月22日から26日までキッズ・パティオ園で行われます。これは年に2回開催される1週間にわたるイベントで、保護者が参加を申込み子どもたちの日常の園生活を見学することが出来ます。園で過ごす時間は子どもたちの日常の生活と成長の大部分を占めており、保護者は普段はその時間を子どもたちと一緒に過ごすことはできません。この事は保護者の皆様にとってとてもつらいことです。なぜならば、子どもたちは日々沢山新しい事を学び、習得しているからです。このような特別な瞬間にその場にいることができないことはつらいことです。

　　　　このことから、キッズ・パティオ園のオープンハウスは、保護者の皆様に子どもたちの園生活と成長への深い洞察を得る機会にしていただくことを目的としています。この機会を積極的にご活用いただき、子どもたちの園での生活を観察し、彼らの成長を覗いて頂きたいと思います。また、子どもたちが園の発展的な取り組みにどのように行動し対応しているのかについて洞察を得ることもできますし、普段の園生活で子どもたちが関わる様々な活動についてもより良く知ることができます。オープンハウスでは子どもたちの活動に自由にご参加ください。そして園に多くのご家族がいらっしゃることで変化する子どもたちの態度にも注目してください。ある子どもはいつになく恥ずかしがるかもしれません。また、他の子どもはいつもと全く違う状況に不安になり泣き叫ぶかもしれません。でも、保護者の皆様には、子どもたちがキッズ・パティオ園で日々習得している全てに誇りを感じていただきお帰りいただければ幸いです。

　　　　参加申込書は園入口にあります。参加希望日時とレベルを必ず記入ください。各家族は選択された日のみ参加が可能で、すべてのレベルを見て頂くこともできます。また、キッズ・パティオプログラムに関心をお持ちのご友人も是非お誘いください。オープンハウスはそのような方にも我々の素晴らしいコミュニティーを直接体験して頂ける唯一の機会となります。

　　　　オープンハウス参加申込みは5月19日（金）に終了します。それ以降の申込みは受けられませんので、是非終了日前までに申し込んでください。よろしくお願いします。

　　　　　　　　　　　敬具　園長　ヤマダ

 Section III

Q.36-Q.38 文章中の(Q.36,37,38)にあてはまる一語を下記リストから選びなさい。一つは該当しません。

1. achieving　　　　　2. inform　　　　　3. observe　　　　　4. considered

正解　　Q.36　2 inform　　　Q.37　3 observe　　　Q.38　1 achieving

解説　　Q.36　オープンハウス開催を [知らせる、通知する] という意味で 2.[inform] が正解です。

Q.37　[園生活を見学する] の意味で 3.[observe] が正解です。Q.38　[learning and ～] につながる進行形 の [習得する] の 1.[achieving] が正解です。

Q.39　お知らせによると、保護者は子どもたちの～に理解が求められます。

1.　　Learning may be stunted by their presence.

2.　　Schedule will be different than normal.

3.　　Friends are welcome to join them at school.

4.　　Behavior may be different than usual.

正解　　4　　Behavior may be different than usual.

解説　　文章で "子どもたちの態度がいつもと違うことに保護者は" とあるので 4.[Behavior may be different than usual.（態度が普段と違う）] が正解です。

Q.40　お知らせによると、オープンハウスの目的で意図されていないのは以下の中でどれですか？

1.　　To provide parents with insight into their child's school life.

2.　　To allow parents an opportunity to evaluate teachers.

3.　　To create an opportunity to peak peek in on their child's development.

4.　　To help parents feel a sense of pride for what their child accomplishes in school.

正解　　2

解説　　2.[To allow parents an opportunity to evaluate teachers.（保護者が先生を評価できる）] は本文では触れられていません。

 Section IV

Writing

二人の先生の電話での会話

スズキ先生：　　ねぇ、今度の日曜日の職員バーベキューには行く？

ヤマナカ先生：行きたいわ。お天気も良さそうだしね。ただお昼にお医者さんの予約が入っているのよ。

スズキ先生：　　大丈夫よ、終わってから来ればいいわよ。おそらく、5時か6時くらいまでいるから。

ヤマナカ先生：遅れて行ったら、ヤマダ園長が気にすると思わない？

スズキ先生：　　病院の予約だもの、理解してくれると思うわよ。なんだったら、ワインでも持ってきたら、他の
　　　　　　　　先生たちも許してくれるわよ！

ヤマナカ先生：いい考えね！赤ワインにするわ！じゃあ、日曜日にね。

Q.41　　　　スズキ先生とヤマナカ先生との内容を英文30字以内でまとめ、Writing専用の解答用紙に書
　　　　　　いてください。

採点基準　　1.Writing専用の解答用紙に記入すること

　　　　　　2.下記の解答が英作文に記載されていること

　　　　　　- どのようなイベントが行われますか？

　　　　　　- ヤマナカ先生が困っていることは何ですか？

　　　　　　- スズキ先生はその問題を解決するのに何を提案しましたか？

　　　　　　＊字数にカンマ、ピリオドは含みません。

Ms. Suzuki is wondering if Ms. Yamanaka will attend the BBQ on Sunday, but Ms. Yamanaka has

a doctor's appointment. Ms. Suzuki suggests if she brings wine, she can arrive late to the BBQ. (30

words)

正解例

第1回　問題

解答解説

リスニング問題　解説（放送問題付き）

 Section I

Dialogue 1 Q.42-Q.46

Principal Yamada:	ヤマダ園長：
Thank you for arranging to meet me, Ms. Yamanaka. I've called you here today because I am incredibly disappointed by the e-mail you sent me.	ヤマナカ先生、会う時間を作って頂きありがとうございました。今日、ここにお呼びしたのは、あなたが私に送ったeメールにとてもがっかりしたからです。
Ms.Yamanaka:	ヤマナカ先生：
I understand, I was just feeling very emotional last Friday　when I sent the e-mail. I'm very upset about my schedule. I have 30 minutes less preparation time compared to other teachers.	わかっています。先週金曜日にメールを送った時はとても感情的になっていました。自分のスケジュールについてとても不満に思っています。他の先生と比べて準備時間が３０分少ないからです。
Principal Yamada:	ヤマダ園長：
Well firstly, please understand that I do not make the teacher's schedules. This is Ms. Suzki's role. Had you informed me of the situation, I would have taken immediate action. Thus, the accusatory tone of your e-mail was completely unwarranted.	そうですか、まず理解してほしいのは、私は先生たちのスケジュールをつくっていません。これはスズキ先生の担当です。状況を事前に教えてくれていたらすぐに対応していました。だから、あなたのeメールの責めるような口調は全く認められません。
Ms. Yamanaka:	ヤマナカ先生：
You are completely right and I apologize for lashing out. I have just been falling apart from stress recently. This is my first year teaching and it's much harder than I thought.	おっしゃる通りです。つっかかってしまったこと謝ります。最近ストレスでボロボロになっていました。保育士になって一年目で思っていた以上に大変です。
Principal Yamada:	ヤマダ園長：
I appreciate the difficulties you are facing as a first year teacher and I am always here to support you, however a professional environment demands respect.	保育士として最初の年で直面して努力をしていることに感謝しますし、私は常にあなたを支えます。でも職場環境はプロとしてお互いに尊敬することが求められます。

Section I

Ms. Yamanaka:	ヤマナカ先生：
I agree completely and promise to work on finding a more positive way to manage my stress and emotions from now on. You have my sincere apologies.	その通りだと思います。今後は自分のストレスや感情をもっと前向きに対応していく方法を見つけるようにします。本当に申し訳ありませんでした。
Principal Yamada:	ヤマダ園長：
Thank you, Ms. Yamanaka. I do hope that things will get easier for you. Please feel free to lean on me for support at anytime, but also know that if I see any repeated disrespectful behavior towards myself or any of our teammates, I will be forced to take disciplinary action.	ヤマナカ先生、ありがとうございます。状況がより楽になるといいですね。助けが必要なときはいつでも私を頼ってくれていいですよ。ただし、私や他の同僚の仲間たちに対し失礼な態度が見られたときは、何か処分をしなければいけなくなります。

Q.42　Who was responsible for arranging the meeting between Principal Yamada and Ms. Yamanaka?

誰がヤマダ園長とヤマナカ先生の話し合いを設定しましたか？

1．Principal Yamada　2．Ms. Yamanaka　3．Ms. Suzuki 4．It is unclear from the passage.

正解　　　1

解説　　　内容から 1.[Principal Yamada(ヤマダ園長)] が正解です。

Q.43　What was Principal Yamada's issue with Ms. Yamanaka ?

ヤマダ園長はヤマナカ先生の何が問題だったのですか？

1. She is struggling as a first year teacher.

2. She has poor communication with Ms. Suzuki.

3. She sent a rude e-mail.

4. She has been lashing out at her students.

正解　　　3

解説　　　内容から 3.[She sent a rude e-mail.(彼女が失礼な e メールを送った)] です。

 Section I

Q.44　Who is responsible for teacher scheduling ?

先生の予定はだれが作成するのですか？

1. Principal Yamada　2. Ms. Yamanaka　3. Ms. Suzuki　4. It is unclear from the passage

正解　　　3

解説　　　内容から 3.[Ms. Suzuki(スズキ先生)] が正解です。

Q.45　Why do you think Ms. Yamanaka is struggling with her role?

ヤマナカ先生は自分の役割になぜ苦労していると思いますか？

1. Due to poor communication with her administrators.

2. She is a first year teacher and is overwhelmed.

3. She has a really challenging class this year.

4. She has poor communication skills.

正解　　　2

解説　　　会話より 2 の [She is a first year teacher and is overwhelmed. (保育士一年目で
いっぱいいっぱいになっています)」 が正解です。

Q.46　How did Principal Yamada solve Ms. Yamanaka's problem?

ヤマダ園長はヤマナカ先生の問題をどう解決しましたか？

1. He had Ms. Suzuki change her schedule.

2. He changed her schedule himself.

3. He had Ms. Yamanaka suggest a schedule change.

4. The problem was not solved in the dialog.

正解　　　4

解説　　　4.[The problem was not solved in the dialog.(対話の中では問題は解決されてない)]
が正解です。

 Section I

Dialogue 2 Q.47-Q.51

Ms. Ishikawa: Principal Yamada, thank you so much for meeting me after　school hours. I have a huge dilemma and I need your advice!	**イシカワさん：** 園長先生、園終了後にお会いいただきまして有難うございます。とても困っていること（ジレンマ）があり、園長先生のアドバイスが必要なのです！
Principal Yamada: It's my pleasure. Your family has been extremely supportive of the school over the past 4 years, so I am happy to return the favor. How can I help you?	**ヤマダ園長：** どうぞ伺いますよ。あなたのご家族はこの4年間園にとても協力的で、そのご好意もお返しできれば喜んで。私にできることはありますか？
Ms. Ishikawa: Well, it's about Ayaka's elementary school. I really want Ayaka to attend an international school, but the problem is my husband. He seems dead set on sending her to public Japanese school.	**イシカワさん：** 実はアヤカの小学校の事なのです。私はアヤカをどうしてもインターナショナルスクールに行かせたいのす。でも、主人が問題なのです。主人は日本の公立学校へ行かせると固く決めているようなのです。
Principal Yamada: I see… it does seem like you are in a difficult position. If I may ask why does your husband have reservations about sending Ayaka to an international elementary school?	**ヤマダ園長：** なるほど、それは難しい立場にいるようですね。うかがってもよろしければ、なぜご主人はアヤカちゃんをインターナショナルスクールに行かせることに難色を示しているのですか？
Ms. Ishikawa: Well, basically he is worried that her Japanese will not be able to develop enough, which will cause many problems for her trying to exist in Japanese society.	**イシカワさん：** そうですね、基本的にはアヤコの日本語が十分上達することが難しいので、日本の社会で生活していく上で多くの問題が起こってくると心配しているのです。

Principal Yamada:

Is he aware that many international schools have Japanese language equivalency programs? Basically, children are studying the exact same Japanese language content as they would be in the public school system.

Ms. Ishikawa:

Wow, I had no idea! I need to tell my husband this right away. I feel so sad for Ayaka because she has been telling us every night that she doesn't want to go to a Japanese school. She really loves being in international schools.

ヤヤマダ園長：

ご主人は、多くのインターナショナルスクールでは日本語の学校と同等の教科課程があることをご存じですか？基本的には子どもたちは公立学校にいるのと全く同じ日本語の内容を勉強しています。

イシカワさん：

まあ、全然知りませんでした！このことをすぐ主人に言わなくては。日本の学校に行きたくないと毎晩私たちに言うものでアヤカがかわいそうでした

彼女はとてもインターナショナルスクールに行きたがっているのです。

Q.47　　Why do you think Principal Yamada agreed to meet with Ms. Ishikawa after school hours?

なぜヤマダ園長は、園が終わった後にイシカワさんに会うことにしたと思いますか？

1. They are old friends.

2. Because the Ishikawas have been so supportive over the years.

3. It's just a normal part of his job.

4. Due to Ms. Ishikawa's work schedule.

正解　　2

解説　　内容から［イシカワ家は今まで4年間、園に協力的だったのでそのご好意をお返ししたい］と園長先生が述べているので 2.[Because the Ishikawas have been so supportive over the years.（なぜならイシカワ家は長年にわたり大変協力的だから）] が正解です。

Section I

Q.48　　What is Ms. Ishikawa's dilemma?

　　　　イシカワさんの困っていること（ジレンマ）は何ですか？

　　　　1. She wants to send Ayaka to Japanese school and her husband does not.

　　　　2. Ayaka does not like her new school.

　　　　3. She wants to send Ayaka to international school and her husband does not.

　　　　4. Ayaka will not express her feeling about where she would like to go to school.

　　　　正解　　　3

　　　　解説　　　内容から 3.[She wants to send Ayaka to international school and her husband does not.(イシカワさんはアヤカをインターナショナルスクールに行かせたいのに、ご主人がそうではない)] からが正解です。

Q.49　　What is one of the Ishikawas' main concerns for Ayaka's elementary school?

　　　　アヤカの小学校に関してお父さんの主な心配事は何ですか？

　　　　1. The type of curriculum available.

　　　　2. The diversity of the student body.

　　　　3. Japanese language support for parents.

　　　　4. The level of Japanese language programming.

　　　　正解　　　4

　　　　解説　　　4.[The level of Japanese language programming.(日本語課程の水準)] が正解です。

Q.50　　How does Principal Yamada assist Ms. Ishikawa with her dilemma?

　　　　ヤマダ園長は困っているイシカワさんをどのように助けてあげますか？

　　　　1. He offers additional information about international schools.

　　　　2. He offers additional information about Japanese public schools.

　　　　3. He offers to meet with Mr. Ishikawa.

　　　　4. He offers to meet with Ayaka.

　　　　正解　　　1

　　　　解説　　　1.[He offers additional information about international schools.(インターナショナルスクールについて追加の情報を教えてあげる)] が正解です。

 Section II

Listening Passage 1 Q.51-Q.55

As parents one of the hardest things to do is finding a balance between loving and protecting our children and giving them the freedom to learn and grow. Overprotecting our children can have vastly negative consequences on child development.

As adults, we may always feel that we know what is best for our children. However, children with healthy neurological systems naturally seek out the sensory input they need on their own. You may find yourself having a natural tendency to say, "No spinning, you may get dizzy," or "Get down from that tree, you may get hurt."

However, when we restrict children from experiencing new sensations of their own free will, they may not develop the senses and motor skills necessary to take risks without getting hurt. Then we, the adults, become the barrier to healthy child development.

Children are natural risk takers. During free play, children learn to manage, control, and even overcome their fears by taking risks. Children who injured themselves by falling from heights between ages five and nine are less likely to be afraid of heights when they are eighteen years old.

On the other hand, if children never go through the process of exposing themselves to new risks, their fear can turn into a phobia.

親として難しい事の一つが子どもたちを愛し守ってあげることと、自由に学び、成長することのバランスを見つけることにあります。過保護は、子どもたちの成長にとても良くない結果をもたらすことがあります。

大人は子どもたちにとって何が一番良いのかを知っていると常に思っています。しかし、健全な精神の持ち主の子どもは自然に必要とする感覚情報を自身で探し求めます。"グルグルと回るのをやめなさい、さもないと目が回りますよ"とか"木から降りなさい、さもないとケガをしますよ"とあなたはごく普通に言っている自分に気が付くかもしれません。

しかしながら、子どもたちの自由な意志による新しい感覚的な経験を奪ってしまうと、ケガをせずに危険を冒すのに必要な判断力と運動神経が育ちません。これでは、我々大人たちが健全な子どもたちの成長の障害になってしまいます。

子どもたちは生まれつきむこうみずなのです。自由に遊びながら、子どもたちは危険を冒して恐さに対応したり、抑えたり更には打ち勝つことを学びます。5歳から9歳の時に高い所から落ちてケガをした子どもたちは１８歳になったとき高さに恐怖を覚えることがより少ないのです。

一方で、新しい危険に自分自身をさらすということが無かった子どもたちは、恐ろしさが恐怖症になることがあります。

In other words, our parental anxiety can become a barrier to children's emotional development as well.

Letting children take risks boosts their confidence. Using a knife to whittle a stick, exploring without an adult, tending a fire, and creating a fort all have one thing in common: there is the risk of injury. Even though letting kids take risks can be scary for parents, these experiences offer considerable reward and value to growing children. When a child takes a risk, such as riding a bike for the first time, it can be frightening.

At the same time, the child is learning to overcome that fear to reach a goal. In the process of learning to ride a bike successfully, the child learns patience, perseverance, and resilience. She learns to keep trying, even when she continues to fall.

Although letting kids take risks may be scary for parents and even children at first, it is an essential part of growing up.

Taking risks allows children to overcome physical challenges and strengthens their senses at the same time. These benefits ultimately make them safer and more resilient in the long run. Risky play also allows children to overcome fears and anxiety and builds strong character.

Children need opportunities to fall and make mistakes in order to become more confident and capable when facing future life challenges.

つまり、親の心配が子どもたちの感情的成長の障害にもなってしまうのです。

子どもたちに危険を冒させることは彼らの自信を高めます。棒をナイフで削ったり、大人なしで探検したり、たき火の番をしたり、砦を造ったりすることに共通項があります。それはケガをする危険があることです。子どもたちに危険を冒させることは親にとって恐いことですが、こういった経験が子どもたちの成長に沢山の褒美と価値をもたらします。子どもたちが危険を冒すとき、たとえば初めて自転車に乗る時とかはゾッとするものです。

それと同時に子どもたちは目的を達成するために恐怖に打ち勝つことを学びます。自転車に上手く乗れるように学ぶ過程で、子どもたちは忍耐、根気強さ、強靭さを身に付けます。転び続けても、挑戦し続けることを学びます。

子どもたちに危険を冒させることは親にとってまた、子どもたちにとっても最初は恐いことかもしれませんが成長する上で極めて重要なことなのです。

危険を冒すことは子どもたちが肉体的な挑戦に打ち勝ちまた、同時に精神力も強くします。このような恩恵は長い目でみれば最終的には子どもたちをより安全に、より強くします。危険な遊びはまた、子どもたちが恐怖や不安に打ち勝つことができるようになり、強い人間を作ります。

子どもたちが将来人生の課題に向かい合う時により大きな自信と能力を身に付けるため、転び失敗する機会が必要なのです。

Q.51　According to the passage, overprotecting children has what effect?

文章の内容から、過保護はどんな結果をもたらしますか？

1. It helps keep children safe.

2. It damages the relationship between child and parent.

3. It increased stress both in children and parents.

4. It has vastly negative consequences on child development.

正解　　4

解説　　4.[It has vastly negative consequences on child development(子どもたちの成
長にとても悪い結果をもたらします)] が正解です。

Q.52　Which of the following was NOT suggested as a risky activity for children?

子たちにとって危険な活動として以下の中、どれが示されていませんか？

1. Riding a bike.

2. Climbing a tree.

3. Tending a fire.

4. Doing self-exploring without an adult.

正解　　2

解説　　2.[Climbing a tree(木登り)] は文章中には具体的な記述はありません。

Q.53　According to the passage, what may happen to a child who is never exposed to new risks?

文章の内容から、新しい危険にさらされることがない子どもたちに起こるかもしれないこと
は何ですか？

1. They may become bored with play.

2. They may begin to have a strained relationship with their parents.

3. Their fears may develop into phobias.

4. They are generally much more mentally healthy by the age of eighteen.

正解　　3

解説　　3.[Their fears may develop into phobias(恐ろしさが恐怖症になるかもしれない)]
です。

Q.54　　The main focus of this passage is...

本文の主たる焦点は・・・

1. Overprotective parents.

2. Identifying risky activities for children.

3. The importance of risk-taking.

4. Respect children's need to explore the world around them.

正解　　　3

解説　　　3.[The importance of risk-taking.(リスクをとる大切さ)] が正解です。

Q.55　　Which of the following was not listed as a benefit of challenging new activities in the

passage?

文中で新しい活動に挑戦する恩恵としてあげられていないのは次のうちのどれですか?

1. The strengthening of sense.

2. A reduction of stress.

3. A boost of self-confidence.

4. The overcoming of fears.

正解　　　2

解説　　　2.[A reduction of stress(ストレスの軽減)] の記述はありません。

 Section II

Listening Passage 2 Q.56-Q.60

Doing homework can be a stressful activity for parents and children alike. Most of the time, children put off finishing their homework because they think it's a tiresome task that will take them hours to finish. Kids naturally want to have fun and will choose playing games over doing tedious assignments any day.

Many things compete for their attention, from TV shows and video games to mobile phones and the Internet.

As a parent, your role is crucial in shaping your child's study and homework habits. You want your child to develop good study habits and to do their homework diligently. However, constantly punishing, nagging, or arguing with your child rarely works for the long term, and such methods only cause more resistance, whining, and complaints.

The following steps can help you to set up a homework routine and that will encourage your child to complete their assignments happily each day.

Step 1: Establish a homework routine on the first day of school.

Creating a regular homework routine that involves when and where assignments should be done is essential. Students greatly benefit from clear structures for completing homework. It's often easier to accomplish tasks when they are tied to certain routines.

　宿題をするというのは、親にとっても子どもたちにとっても同様にストレスがかかるものです。
宿題を終えるまで何時間もかかる面倒な作業と思いだいたい子どもたちは先延ばしにします
子どもたちは当然楽しいことをしたいと思っているので、いつでもうんざりする宿題をするよりもゲームで遊ぶことを選びます。

　テレビ、ビデオゲームから携帯電話、インターネットまで彼らにはたくさんの誘惑があります。

　子どもたちの勉強や宿題を習慣づける上で、親としてのあなたの役割は重要です。あなたは子どもたちに勉強の習慣を身につけ、宿題を真面目にして欲しいのです。しかしながら、子どもたちに対してたえず罰したり、小言を言ったり、言い争うのは長い目でみて何の効果もありませんし、そのようなやり方では、さらなる反抗、不平不満、文句のもとになるだけです。

　以下の方法は宿題を習慣づけ、子どもたちが宿題を毎日楽しく終えるように仕向けます。

方法１：学校初日に、宿題を日課にすることを決める。

　いつ、どこで宿題をするかを含めた規則的な日課を作り上げることが重要です。生徒は宿題を終える明確な方法に多いに助けられます。日課にすることで多くはより簡単に達成できます。

Section I

Step 2: Find a suitable space in your home where your child can do homework.

The right location depends on your child's preferences. Some kids find it comfortable to work in their rooms, where the quiet ambiance promotes concentration. Others are easily distracted by playthings in their bedroom, so are likely to perform better at a location with fewer distractions, such as the dining room table.

Ask your child about where they'll feel most relaxed. Ideally, the location should be quiet, clean, and free of distraction, allowing your child to stay focused.

Step 3: Create a homework center.

After identifying the location most conducive to completing homework, the next step is to set it up as a homework center. Ensure that the workspace is roomy enough to accommodate all necessary materials for doing assignments. Find out the types of supplies your child typically uses, and provide all basic supplies, including pencils, pens, papers, colored markers, and rulers. A dictionary, thesaurus, and calculator may also be necessary.

Step 4: Choose a homework time.

It's essential to establish a particular time for doing homework every day. Your child should be able to get used to this schedule until it becomes a normal daily routine. It's also good to do homework after dinner when children feel full and their energy levels have been replenished.

方法２：家の中で子どもたちが宿題をする適切な場所を見つける。

最適の場所は子どもの好みによります。ある子どもは自分の部屋が心地良いと感じ、静かな状況が集中力を高めてくれます。ある子どもたちは自分の寝室にあるおもちゃに容易に気が散らされるので、おもちゃがほとんど置かれていない食卓テーブルなどが良い場所に思われます。

あなたの子どもに最も落ち着くことができる場所を聞いてみてください。理想を言えば、子どもが集中できる静かで清潔で気が散らない場所が良いでしょう。

方法３：宿題センターをつくる。

宿題を終えるのに最適の場所が分かったら、次はそこを宿題センターに決めることです。
そこが宿題をするのに必要な道具をすべて置くことができる十分な広さがあることを確認してください。子どもがよく使う必需品を探し、全ての必要最低限の文房具、例えば鉛筆、ペン、紙、色マーカー、定規などを準備しましょう。辞書、百科辞典、計算機も必要かもしれません。

方法４：宿題時間を決める。

毎日宿題をする時間を決めることが大切です。通常の日課になるまで、子どもはこの予定に慣れることが必要です。また、子どもたちが満腹で、活力レベルが最高の夕食後に宿題をすることもいいでしょう。

However, avoid doing assignments later in the evening, because your child may feel too exhausted to think.	ただ、あまり夜遅くに宿題をするのは、子どもは考えることに疲れすぎてしまうかもしれないので避けたほうがよいでしょう。
Step 5: Include breaks. Working on assignments continuously can quickly drain your child physically and mentally. Let him decide when he'd like to take a break, and include his chosen break periods in the daily homework schedule.	**方法5：休憩を入れる。** 宿題をし続けることは、肉体的にも精神的にも子どもを早く消耗させます。子どもにいつ休憩をとりたいか決めさせ、日々の宿題予定表に選んだ休憩時間を入れましょう。
Step 6: Offer rewards. Mark your homework calendar for each day of successful completion of assignments, and offer rewards and incentives on certain days. Access to electronics, playtime with friends, or the purchase of new video game at the end of the month are all great incentives.	**手順6：ご褒美をあげる。** 宿題を終えることができた日を宿題予定表にマークしましょう。そして一定の日数にご褒美や励みとなるものを与えましょう。電子機器をさせたり、友達と遊ぶ時間をつくったり、月末に新しいビデオゲームの購入など、全てがとても励みとなるものです。

Q.56　　When should a child's homework routine be established？

子どもの宿題日課はいつ作るべきですか？

1. After the child has fully settled into their new classroom.

2. Before the new school year begins.

3. After the first week of school.

4. On the first day of school.

正解　　4

解説　　4.[On the first day of school(学校の最初の日)] が正解です。

Q.57　What is the best way to determine the location of your child's homework space?

子どもが宿題をする部屋を決める最も良い方法は何ですか？

1. Parents should use their best judgment and chose the space on their own.

2. By consulting your child about their preferences.

3. By consulting with the child's teacher about their learning style.

4. Via parent and teacher collaboration.

正解　　2

解説　　2.[By consulting your child about their preferences(子どもにどこが良いか聞く)]
　　　　が正解です。

Q.58　Which of the following is NOT offered as positive homework incentive?

積極的に宿題をする気持ちにさせるものとしてあげられていないのは以下のうちどれ

ですか？

1. A special family dinner.

2. Access to electronics.

3. A new video game.

4. Time with friends.

正解　　1

解説　　1.[A special family dinner(家族との特別ディナー)]は触れられていません。

Q.59　Which of the following would the author be likely to NOT recommend ?

著者が薦めていないものは以下のうちどれですか？

1. Ensure that your child's homework center is well supplied.

2. Allow time for regular breaks while doing homework.

3. Allow your child the freedom to choose where they want to do their homework.

4. Make frequent changes to homework routines to avoid children getting bored.

正解　　4

解説　　4.[Make frequent changes to homework routines to avoid children getting
　　　　bored（子どもたちが飽きないように、宿題日課を頻繁に変える)]が正解です。

Q.60　　　What is the best choice for a title for the passage?

　　　　　このパッセージの主題として最適な選択は以下のうちどれですか？

　　　　　1. The Importance of Homework

　　　　　2. Helping Your Child Develop Positive Homework Habits

　　　　　3. Why Your Child Hates Homework

　　　　　4. Helping with Homework

正解　　　2

解説　　　2.[Helping Your Child Develop Positive Homework Habits(子どもが積極的に宿題
　　　　　をする習慣をつけさせる)] です。

 Section II

Listening Passage 3 Q.61-Q.66

The International Baccalaureate Program, or IB Program for short was founded in Geneva, Switzerland in 1968 where it is also headquartered. The IB offers programming for Primary, Middle School, and High School levels. In order to host these programs, schools must go through a rigorous accreditation process where the IB organization will evaluate everything from school facilities, health and sanitation, to teacher training and effectiveness.

The IB curriculum is the world's first curriculum designed specifically for the international context and international schools. The IB curriculum values diversity, global mindedness, and diplomacy. The IB approach is completely different from traditional educational methods. There are no examinations, but instead students are assessed on their ability to apply their knowledge in realistic and practical ways. Throughout the year students develop a portfolio of their work that can contain projects, experiments, and community work on which they will be assessed. The IB diploma is highly recognized and coveted by universities around the globe due to its rigor and practical application towards both university study and real life situations.

国際バカロレア・プログラム（略称 IB）は1968 年にスイス、ジュネーブで設立され、ここが本部にもなっています。IB は小学校、中学校、高等学校レベル向けのプログラムを提供します。これらのプログラムを受けるためには、学校は厳しい認定プロセスを経なければなりません。IB は学校の設備、健康衛生設備から先生の養成、実効性まで審査します。

IB 教育課程は特に国際分野および国際学校（インターナショナルスクール）向けに作られた世界で初めての教育課程で、多様性、国際感覚性、外交性を重んじます。IB の取り組み方は、従来の教育方法とは全く異なります。試験はありませんが、代わりに生徒は現実的で実用的な方法で彼らの知識を応用する能力で評価されます。年間を通し生徒は研究課題、実地経験、社会活動を含む成果について評価ツールをつくりあげ、これらが評価されるのです。IB 修了証書は、その厳しさと、大学での研究や実生活の状況に実用的に応用できることから世界中の大学で高く評価され熱望されています。

　　　無断転載・複写を禁じます

Section II

Q.61　　Which of the following year groups does IB support?

年齢別グループで IB が支援しているのは以下のうちどれですか？

1. Only Primary School years.

2. Only Middle School years.

3. Only High School years.

4. The IB supports Primary, Middle School, and High School.

正解　　　4

解説　　　4.[The IB supports Primary, Middle School, and High School (IB は小学校、中学校、高等学校を支援する)] が正解です。

Q.62　　According to the passage, how is the IB program radically different from traditional educational approaches?

パッセージから、IB プログラムが従来の教育的取り組みと根本的に異なることは？

1. There are no textbooks.

2. The teacher to student ratio is much lower.

3. There are no exams.

4. Classes take place in non-traditional classroom environments.

正解　　　3

解説　　　3.[There are no exams(試験がない)] が正解です。

Q.63　　Where was the IB program founded?

IB プログラムはどこで設立されましたか？

1. Sweden

2. Germany

3. Norway

4. Switzerland

正解　　　4

解説　　　4.[Switzerland(スイス)] です。

Section II

Q.64　Which of the following was not mentioned as a curriculum value of the IB Program?

IB プログラム教育課程の価値として述べられていないのは以下のうちどれですか？

1. Leadership

2. Diversity

3. Diplomacy

4. Global Mindedness

正解　　　1

解説　　　1.[Leadership(リーダーシップ)] は本文で述べられていません。

Q.65　Based on the passage, do you feel the IB program is a quality approach to education?

パッセージから、IB プログラムは教育に対し素晴らしい取り組みだと感じますか？

1. Yes, because IB diplomas are highly desired from universities around the world.

2. Yes, because IB students must go through rigorous testing standards.

3. No, because IB students have a difficult time relating their knowledge to the real world.

4. It is unclear from the passage.

正解　　　1

解説　　　1.[Yes, because IB diplomas are highly desired from universities around the world. (IB 修了証書は世界中の大学から高く願望されている)] が正解です。

Q.66　Which of the following is TRUE about the IB Program?

IB プログラムで正しいのは以下のうちどれですか？

1. Students must pass a rigorous exam to qualify for the IB curriculum.

2. It was the first curriculum developed specifically for international schools.

3. There are no projects in the IB Program.

4. The IB program has been around for less than 25 years.

正解　　　2

解説　　　2.[It was the first curriculum developed specifically for international schools.(特に国際学校（インターナショナルスクール）のために開発された最初の教育課程である)] が正解です。

　　　　無断転載・複写を禁じます

第2回　問題

解答解説

Level Pre-1 第2回　解答

Q.1	2
Q.2	4
Q.3	3
Q.4	3
Q.5	1
Q.6	4
Q.7	2
Q.8	4
Q.9	1
Q.10	2
Q.11	4
Q.12	3
Q.13	2
Q.14	1
Q.15	2
Q.16	3
Q.17	2
Q.18	3
Q.19	4
Q.20	1

Q.21	3
Q.22	4
Q.23	1
Q.24	2
Q.25	3
Q.26	2
Q.27	4
Q.28	4
Q.29	3
Q.30	1
Q.31	3
Q.32	2
Q.33	4
Q.34	1
Q.35	3
Q.36	2
Q.37	4
Q.38	1
Q.39	4
Q.40	2

Q.42	2
Q.43	1
Q.44	4
Q.45	1
Q.46	3
Q.47	3
Q.48	1
Q.49	3
Q.50	4
Q.51	1
Q.52	3
Q.53	3
Q.54	3
Q.55	2
Q.56	3
Q.57	4
Q.58	2
Q.59	1
Q.60	3
Q.61	3
Q62	4
Q.63	2
Q.64	3
Q.65	1
Q.66	2

Q.41

Ken asked Tom about his winter plans. Tom is going to go surfing in Honolulu, so Ken will give Tom information about a surfing instructor. (30 words)

 Section I

Q.1　正解　2　Not only

解説　[タロウはパーティーを楽しんだだけではなく、新しい多くの友人も出来た] という内容ですから 2.[Not only][～だけではなく] が正解です。1.[definitely] は [明確に]、2.[consequently] は [結果として] という意味です。

Q.2　正解　4　get rid of

解説　[リエちゃんは臭くなった古い上履きを捨てるべきです] という内容ですから 4.[get rid of(捨てる)] が正解です。1.[get free of ～] は [(義務や負担) に関して自由である]、2.[get free from ～] は [(いやなことや苦痛) から自由になる]、3.[ridden] は [ride の過去分詞] です。

Q.3　正解　3　throughout

解説　[キッズパティオ園では一年を通して、避難訓練をしています] という内容ですから 3.[throughout(通して)] が正解です。

Q.4　正解　3　ask for seconds

解説　[BBQ は食べ放題ですから、おなかがまだすいていたら遠慮なくおかわりをしてください] という内容ですから 3. [ask for seconds(おかわりをする)] が正解です。1.[alteratives] は [代替案]、4.[duplicates] は [複製] という意味です。

Q.5　正解　1　put out

解説　[今朝は大変な大雨になりそうなので、皆さんのために傘立てを出しておきましょう] という内容ですから 1.[put out(取り出す)] が正解です。なお、2.[put up] は [put up with][我慢する] でよく使われ,[put up] は [宿泊する、傘をさす、告知などを掲示する] など、様々な意味となります。

Q.6　正解　4　stable

解説　[妻の体調がまだ安定していないので、病院から出られません] という内容ですから 4. [stable(安定している)] が正解です。1.[vulnerable] は [傷つきやすい] という意味です。

Section I

Q.7　正解　2　　　due date

解説　[出産は 9 月が予定日ですので、おそらく 8 月末にお休みを取る必要があります] という内容ですから2.[due date(予定日)] が正解です 1.[birthing day] は [出産日]、3.[commencement date] は [開始日、施行日] という意味です。

Q.8　正解　4　　　bothered by

解説　[エリちゃんは本当に騒音で悩んでいるみたいです。いつも耳を覆って叫びます] という内容ですから 4. [bothered by(悩まされる)] が正解です 1.[consume] は [消費する]、2.[belittle] は [見くびる] という意味です。

Q.9　正解　1　　　That something has improved.

解説　[以前よりはるかに良いという表現はどういう意味ですか？] という内容ですから [That something has improved.(ある事が改善している)] が正解です

Q.10　正解　2　　　To continue an action when facing challenges

解説　[持ちこたえるとはどういう意味ですか？] という内容ですから [To continue an action when facing challenges.(困難に面していても対応を続けること)] が正解です。

 **Section I**

Dialogue 1 Q.11-Q.15　　　　　　保護者(マリコさんとジュディさん)二人の会話

マリコ：　こんにちはジュディ、お帰りなさい! 会いたかったのよ! その子が新しい赤ちゃん?

ジュディ：　ありがとうございます。 はい、私たちのいたずらな小さなジェームズです。彼で Q.11) 手一杯です。

マリコ：　でしょうね!でも 2 人目の子だから今回は Q.12) ゆったりとした気持ちのはずだけどね。

ジュディ：　ええ、私たちは最初の子ではかなり Q.13) 気疲れしたけど、今回は経験があったので大分楽だったわ。

マリコ：　それは良かった! 食事の方はどう?

ジュディ：　一歩一歩。まだ母乳育児中だけど、だいたいあと 1 ヶ月以内に固形食を Q.14) 始めてみる計画よ。

マリコ：　それまで待てないわよね。Q.15) 授乳は本当にエネルギーを全部奪ってしまうからね。

ジュディ：　その通りね! その日を今か今かと待ってる!

マリコ　：　全くね。まだまだ時間があるわね。早くそうなるよう祈りましょう!

Q.11　　　正解　　　4　　　handful
　　　　　解説　　　[彼で手一杯です]という内容ですから 4.[handful(手一杯)] が正解です。

Q.12　　　正解　　　3　　　relaxed
　　　　　解説　　　[ゆったりとした気持ちで]という内容ですから 3.[relaxed(ゆったりとした気持ちで)]が正解です。2.[belabor]は[不必要に長く論じる]、4.[tense]は[緊張した]という意味です。

Q.13　　　正解　　　2　　　stressed
　　　　　解説　　　[初めの子ときは大変だった]という内容ですから 2.[stressed(気疲れ)]が正解です。3.[intolerant]は[耐えられないで]という意味です。

Q.14　　　正解　　　1　　　introduce
　　　　　解説　　　始めてみるという内容ですから、1.[introduce(始める)]が正解です。

Q.15　　　正解　　　2　　　nursing
　　　　　解説　　　[授乳は]という内容ですから、2.[Nursing(授乳)]が正解です。3. [pasteurize]は[殺菌をおこなう]という言う意味です。

 Section II

Dialogue 2 Q.16-Q.20　　　　　保護者と園長の電話会話

保護者：　私たちはあなたの園がとても気に入りましたので、息子をすぐにQ 16) 入園させたいと思います。

園長：　　それを聞いて本当にうれしいです。登録簿で席の空きがあるかを、Q.17) 再度確認したいので少しお待ちください。

保護者：　ありがとうございます！空きがあるとよいのですが。

園長：　　ありそうです！お子さんの Q.18) 発達状況について もうすこし教えてください。

保護者：　まず、彼女は 18 ヶ月で話し始め、1 年間固形食を食べています。ただ、指の細かな運動能力はまだないので、おそらくボタンをはめたりする助けを必要とすると思います。

園長：　　わかりました、問題ありません。あとは、健康保険のコピーを提出し、入園料をお納めいただくだけです。それで、申し込み手続き Q.20) を完了と致します。

Q.16　　　正解　　3　　　　enroll
　　　　　解説　　[入学手続きをしたい、入園する] という内容ですから3.[enroll(入学手続きをする、入園する)] が正解です。

Q.17　　　正解　　2　　　　double check
　　　　　解説　　再確認したいということですから 2.[double check(再確認する)] が正解です。
　　　　　　　　　3.[corroborate] は [確証する]、4.[authenticate] は [証明する] という意味です。

Q.18　　　正解　　3　　　　development
　　　　　解説　　会話の内容から、発育状況を聞いていますので、3.[development(発育状況)] が正解です。1.[enlargement] は [拡大]、2.[maturity] は [成熟]、4.[evolution] は [進化] です。

Q.19　　　正解　　4　　　　most probably
　　　　　解説　　会話の内容から、4.[most probably(おそらくは)] が正解です。

Q.20　　　正解　　1　　　　process
　　　　　解説　　[手続き] という内容ですから 1.[process(手続き)] が正解です。

 Section III

Listening Passage 1 Q.21-Q.35

The Power of Outdoor Classroom as a Catalyst for Creativity
創造性の触媒としての屋外教室の力 （英文理解のための補助和訳）

貴方が創造性について考えるとき、何が頭に浮かぶでしょうか？多くの私たちにとってそれは芸術です：描画、絵画、文書、またはダンス。それらは明らかに創造努力ではありますが、創造性は全体的な分野にわたって考えること、学ぶための方法でもあります。創造的であることということは、結びつきをつくり、異なる観点から物事を見るということです。それは問題解決、柔軟な思考、そして戦略化を含みます。

おそらく今まで以上に社会として、私たちは問題解決をするとき、様々な状況に適応するとき、効果的に他とのコミュニケーンをとるときに創造性を使うことができる人々を必要としています。私たちは客観的でよりよく策を考え、それを実行でき、新しい方法を試しながら表現できる人々を必要としています。（与えられた情報を、原因や理由を積極的に使って分析し、評価できる人。）

他のスキルと同じように創造的に考える能力は、育成し使うことで成長します。どのようにして子どもたちが創造的に動ける機会を提供できるでしょうか？定期的に自然の中、屋外で過ごすことは、創造性を高めるための検証済みの方法の一つです。自然は効果的に子どもたちを実践的な遊びへいざない、子どもたちの創造的な問題解決力を養い、また、実際に乗り越えなければならない課題に直面させてくれます。自然の野外教室は、子どもたちが人間の進化や最新の脳研究と同等の方法で効果的に学ぶ創造的な実験室です。

進化化学は脳が問題を解決するように設計されていると報告しています。脳の研究では、体が動いているときに頭が最も効果的に機能するとしています。脳は動かず座っている状態で記憶するようには設計されていません。証拠は明白です：有酸素運動は最高の能力を発揮するように脳を身体的に改造します。私たちの脳は、私たちが動いていないならば、何かを覚える必要がないと認識するのです。それでは、運動が学習に不可欠だとするならば、従来の教育環境（屋内の教室）はどのように理想的な学習を支援するのでしょうか？専門家の中には、頭脳が得意とすることと正反対の教育環境を作りたいのであれば、（従来の）教室のようなものを設計するだろうと考える人もいます。

反対に、子どもの動きを促したり、選択機会を十分に与えることができる、熟考され、自然に満ちた屋外教室では柔軟で創造的な思考を支えます。

 Section III

自然の屋外教室は強い脳の発達を提供します。それらは遊びや学習に理想的な場所です。このような空間は子どもに、調査、問題解決、思考、再考、そして世の中がどのように動いているかについての概念と理解を洗練するための多くの機会を与えます。

創造性を支える屋外における大人の役割は過小評価されるべきではありません。教育者が、子どもたちが定期的に屋外で過ごす時間の価値、及び生徒の学習支援をする上での重要な役割の価値を理解したときに、創造性は花開きます。難しい作業を手助けする、遊びの中に入る、子どもたちに率先するよう励ます、そして見守ることが最良の援助である時など、これらの頃合いを見計らい、臨機応変に決断するのが大人の役割なのです。

Q.21-Q.24

Q.21	正解	3	endeavors
	解説	3.[endeavors(努力)] が正解です。	
Q.22	正解	4	domains
	解説	4.[domains(分野)] が正解です。	
Q.23	正解	1	connections
	解説	1. [connections(結び付ける)] が正解です。	
Q.24	正解	2	perspectives
	解説	2. [perspectives(観点)] が正解です。	

Q.25-Q.29

Q.25	正解	3	As a society
	解説	3.[As a society(社会として)] が正解です。	
Q.26	正解	2	by trying out
	解説	2. [by trying out(試しながら)] が正解です。	
Q.27	正解	4	How can we
	解説	4. [How can we(どのようにして)] が正解です。	
Q.28	正解	4	are compatible with
	解説	4.[are compatible with(同等)] が正解です。	
Q.29	正解	3	As far as
	解説	3. [As far as(関する限り)] が正解です。	

 Section III

Q.30 -Q.35

Q.30　下の単語リストから（　　　）に入る最も適切なものを選びなさい。
　　　　正解　　　1　　　　　essential
　　　　解説　　　1. [essential(不可欠)] が正解です。

Q.31　4 段落目と 5 段落目によると、学習について正しくないものはどれですか？
　　　　正解　　　3
　　　　解説　　　3.[Movement should be minimized to reduce student distractions.(動き回ることは
　　　　　　　　　生徒の注意散漫になるため最小限に抑えなければならない)] が正解です。

Q.32　3 段落目で使われた語句 ” time-tested” の意味は何ですか？
　　　　正解　　　2
　　　　解説　　　2.[Something that has been proven true over a long period.(長期間で正しいと証明
　　　　　　　　　されたこと)] が正解です

Q.33　6 段落目で使われた” underestimated” の同義語は下記のうちどれですか？
　　　　正解　　　4
　　　　解説　　　4.[undervalued(過小評価された)] が正解です

Q.34　6 段落目で削除された言葉の順序で正しいものはどれですか？
　　　　正解　　　1　　⑤ - ③ - ② - ① - ④ - ⑥
　　　　解説　　　1. [when educators understand the value of(教育者がその価値を理解した時)] が
　　　　　　　　　正解です。(* 答えの選択肢の頭文字は小文字で記載されています)

Q.35　パッセージの内容から動き回ることの利点は何と述べられていますか？
　　　　正解　　　3
　　　　解説　　　3.[It helps the mind to operate more effectively(頭がより効果的に働きます)] が正
　　　　　　　　　解です

Listening Passage 2　Q.36-Q.40

キッズパティオ園よりファミリーピクニックに関するおたより

保護者の皆様

秋も近づき、ファミリーピクニックの日程のQ.36）お知らせができ嬉しく思います。毎年恒例のキッズ パティオ ファミリーピクニックは10月20日（金）午後1時から午後4時まで開催され、ご家族参加のイベントとなります。広尾と目黒の両方のキャンパスよりこの特別な家族イベントに参加できます。このキャンパス合同イベントは目黒キャンパスのQ.37）真向かいにある目黒公園で開催されます。TIKは、すべての広尾キャンパスのご家族のために、イベント会場への往復の無料バスサービスを提供します。

キッズ パティオ ファミリーピクニックはポットラックスタイル（持ち寄り）のピクニックになり、ご家族には公園でQ.38）ゆったりとしたランチを楽しみながら美しい景色を堪能していただけます。TIKの子どもたちはピクニックの間、ゲームや活動に参加し、宝探しに参加することができます。これは、子どもと親が一緒に様々なスポーツ活動に一緒に参加する運動会形式の催しとなります。保護者の皆様はどうぞ子どもたちのこれらの楽しい催しに参加できるような服装でいらしてください。

持ちよりについては、各ご家族には何かおやつかお料理を持ってきていただきますようお願いいたします。各家族は10-20人が十分に食べる量を持ってきていただきますようお願いします。紙皿、カップ、フォーク、ナイフ、箸、そして飲み物はキッズパテイオより提供します。アレルギー制限のある子どもがいるため、ナッツや生卵を含む食品はご遠慮ください。ご家族がピクニックの間に座るために敷物をご持参ください。また、宝探し用のキャンディの寄付も受付けています。宝探し用に何か良いものを寄付したい方は、いずれかの園の事務所のお届けください。

イベント当日、12:40にキッズ パティオ目黒に家族全員集合予定です。キッズ パティオ目黒から午12時50分に目黒公園に向います。午後のプログラムのお子様ご家族も、12:40にキッズ パティオ目黒に到着するようにお願いします。12:40までに到着できないご家族は、直接公園にいらしてください。公園の地図は後日配布します。

雨天の場合は、10月27日（金）の午後1時から午後4時に変更します。両日雨であれば、皆さまのご予定や、お仕事のご予定を何度も変更していただくことは難しいと思いますので、残念ながら、中止とします。それを念頭に置いて、よい天気に恵まれますよう期待しておりますし、今年の素晴らしいイベントを楽しみにしています！

園長　ヤマダ

Q.36-Q.38
Q.36,Q.37,Q.38 に入る最も正しいものを下記から選びなさい。答えのうち一つはどれにもあてはまりません。

Q.36　　正解　　2　　　　announce
　　　　解説　　2.［announce(お知らせする)］という意味です。

Q.37　　正解　　4　　　　directly
　　　　解説　　4.［directly(真正面)］という意味です。

Q.38　　正解　　1　　　　leisurely
　　　　解説　　1.［leisurely(ゆったりと、贅沢に)］という意味です。

Q.39　　手紙によると、20 日が雨天の場合はどうなりますか？
　　　　正解　　4　　　The event will be rescheduled only once.
　　　　解説　　4.［The event will be rescheduled only once.(イベントは一度のみ予定が変更されます（延期される))］が正解です

Q.40　　手紙によると、次のうちどれがイベント（家族ピクニック）中の活動として述べられていませんか？
　　　　正解　　2　　　Group singing
　　　　解説　　2.［Group singing(合唱)］が正解です

 Section IV

Writing

Q.41　　　　対話を読んで対話の内容を 30 ワードでまとめなさい。

Ms. Suzuki:　　　今年の冬休みはどこにいきますか?

Ms. Yamanaka:　今週の土曜にホノルルにいきます。とても楽しみです。

Ms. Suzuki:　　　わぁー、エキゾチックですね。ホノルルで何する予定ですか?

Ms. Yamanaka:　実はサーフィンのレッスンを受けるつもりです。ずーと習いたいと思っていました。

Ms. Suzuki:　　　ワイキキビーチにすごいサーフィンのインストラクターを知っています。連絡先を教えましょう

Ms. Yamanaka:　わぁー、すごい!

Q.41

採点基準

1. Writing 専用の用紙に記入すること

2. Ms. SuzukiとMs. Yamanakaの対話の内容が正しく説明されていること

3. 文法、スペリング、字数が正確であること

*字数にカンマ、ピリオドは含みません。

> 正解例:Ms. Suzuki asked Ms. Yamanaka about his winter plans. Ms. Yamanaka is going to go surfing in Honolulu, so Ms. Suzuki will give Ms. Yamanaka information about a surfing instructor. (30 words)

第2回　問題

解答解説

リスニング問題　解説（放送問題付き）

 Section I

Dialogue 1 Q.42-Q.46

Principal Yamada:	**ヤマダ園長：**
Thank you for arranging to meet me, Ms. Yamanaka. I've called you here today because I am incredibly disappointed by the e-mail you sent me.	ヤマナカ先生、会う時間を作って頂きありがとうございました。今日、ここにお呼びしたのは、あなたが私に送ったeメールにとてもがっかりしたからです。
Ms.Yamanaka:	**ヤマナカ先生：**
I understand, I was just feeling very emotional last Friday when I sent the e-mail. I'm very upset about my schedule. I have 30 minutes less preparation time compared to other teachers.	わかっています。先週金曜日にメールを送った時はとても感情的になっていました。自分のスケジュールについてとても不満に思っています。他の先生と比べて準備時間が３０分少ないからです。
Principal Yamada:	**ヤマダ園長：**
Well firstly, please understand that I do not make the teacher's schedules. This is Ms. Suzki's role. Had you informed me of the situation, I would have taken immediate action. Thus, the accusatory tone of your e-mail was completely unwarranted.	そうですか、まず理解してほしいのは、私は先生たちのスケジュールをつくっていません。これはスズキ先生の担当です。状況を事前に教えてくれていたらすぐに対応していました。だから、あなたのeメールの責めるような口調は全く認められません。
Ms. Yamanaka:	**ヤマナカ先生：**
You are completely right and I apologize for lashing out. I have just been falling apart from stress recently. This is my first year teaching and it's much harder than I thought.	おっしゃる通りです。つっかかってしまったこと謝ります。最近ストレスでボロボロになっていました。保育士になって一年目で思っていた以上に大変です。
Principal Yamada:	**ヤマダ園長：**
I appreciate the difficulties you are facing as a first year teacher and I am always here to support you, however a professional environment demands respect.	保育士として最初の年で直面して努力をしていることに感謝しますし、私は常にあなたを支えます。でも職場環境はプロとしてお互いに尊敬することが求められます。

Principal Yamada:	ヤマダ園長：

Principal Yamada:

I appreciate the difficulties you are facing as a first year teacher and I am always here to support you, however a professional environment demands respect.

Ms. Yamanaka:

I agree completely and promise to work on finding a more positive way to manage my stress and emotions from now on. You have my sincere apologies.

Principal Yamada: Thank you, Ms. Yamanaka. I do hope that things will get easier for you. Please feel free to lean on me for support at any time, but also know that if I see any repeated disrespectful behavior towards myself or any of our teammates, I will be forced to take disciplinary action.

ヤマダ園長：

保育士として最初の年で直面して努力をしていることに感謝しますし、私は常にあなたを支えます。
でも職場環境はプロとしてお互いに尊敬することが求められます。

ヤマナカ先生：

その通りだと思います。今後は自分のストレスや感情をもっと前向きに対応していく方法を見つけるようにします。本当に申し訳ありませんでした。

ヤマダ園長：

ヤマナカ先生、ありがとうございます。状況がより楽になるといいですね。助けが必要なときはいつでも私を頼ってくれていいですよ。ただし、私や他の同僚の仲間たちに対し失礼な態度が見られたときは、何か処分をしなければいけなくなります。

Q.42　What did Ms. Yamanaka do to make Principal Yamada disappointed?
ヤマナカ先生は何でヤマダ園長をがっかりさせたのですか？

1.　She used too much time to prepare.
2.　She complained to him about her job in a message.
3.　She was 30 minutes late to class.
4.　She gave him a schedule that he didn't like.

正解　2

解説　2.[She complained to him about her job in a message.（文中で仕事について不平を言ったか ら)］が正解です。

Q.43　According to Principal Yamada, what should have Ms. Yamanaka done about her situation?
　　　ヤマダ園長によれば、ヤマナカ先生は状況にどのように対応すればよかったのですか？

　　　1.　　Discussed it with him.

　　　2.　　Written an email to Ms. Suzuki.

　　　3.　　Changed her schedule.

　　　4.　　Gone home early on Friday.

　　　正解　　1

　　　解説　　1.[Discussed it with him.(先に打ち合わせをすべき)] が正解です。

Q.44　How does Ms. Yamanaka feel about her first year teaching ?
　　　ヤマナカ先生は初年度教えてみてどのように感じていましたか？

　　　1.　　It's a lot of fun.

　　　2.　　She doesn't enjoy her job.

　　　3.　　The children are noisy.

　　　4.　　It is very stressful.

　　　正解　　4

　　　解説　　4.[It is very stressful. 強いストレスになっている）] が正解で。

Q.45　What is Ms. Yamanaka going to do to make the situation better?
　　　ヤマナカ先生はどのように状況を改善させますか？

　　　1.　　Try to control her emotions better

　　　2.　　Get professional help

　　　3.　　Come to work earlier

　　　4.　　Get an easier job

　　　正解　　1

　　　解説　　1.[Try to control her emotions better(感情をより良く制御する)] が正解です。

Q.46　　What will happen if Ms. Yamanaka doesn't respect her boss in the future?

今後、ヤマナカ先生が上司に敬意を払わなければどうなりますか？

1.　　　The school will fire her.

2.　　　Her boss will support her.

3.　　　She will be punished.

4.　　　Her boss will disrespect her.

正解　　3

解説　　3.[She will be punished.(彼女は罰を受ける)] が正解です。

Dialogue2 Q.47- Q.51

Ms. Ishikawa: Principal Yamada, thank you so much for meeting me　after school hours. I have a huge dilemma and I need your advice!	**イシカワさん：** 園長先生、園終了後にお会いいただきまして有難うございます。とても困っていること（ジレンマ）があり、園長先生のアドバイスが必要なのです！
Principal Yamada: It's my pleasure. Your family has been extremely supportive of the school over the past 4 years, so I am happy to return the favor. How can I help you?	**ヤマダ園長：** どうぞ伺いますよ。あなたのご家族はこの4年間園にとても協力的で、そのご好意もお返しできれば喜んで。私にできることはありますか？
Ms. Ishikawa: Well, it's about Ayaka's elementary school. I really want Ayaka to attend an international school, but the problem is my husband. He seems dead set on sending her to public Japanese school.	**イシカワさん：** 実はアヤカの小学校の事なのです。私はアヤカをどうしてもインターナショナルスクールに行かせたいのす。でも、主人が問題なのです。主人は日本の公立学校へ行かせると固く決めているようなのです。
Principal Yamada: I see… it does seem like you are in a difficult position. If I may ask why does your husband have reservations about sending Ayaka to an international elementary school?	**ヤマダ園長：** なるほど、それは難しい立場にいるようですね。伺ってもよろしければ、なぜご主人はアヤカちゃんをインターナショナルスクールに行かせることに難色を示しているのですか？
Ms. Ishikawa: Well, basically he is worried that her Japanese will not be able to develop enough, which will cause many problems for her trying to exist in Japanese society.	**イシカワさん：** そうですね、基本的にはアヤカの日本語が十分上達することが難しいので、日本の社会で生活していく上で多くの問題が起こってくると心配しているのです。

Principal Yamada:

Is he aware that many international schools have Japanese language equivalency programs? Basically, children are studying the exact same Japanese language content as they would be in the public school system.

Ms. Ishikawa:

Wow, I had no idea! I need to tell my husband this right away. I feel so sad for Ayaka because she has been telling us every night that she doesn't want to go to a Japanese school. She really loves being in international schools.

ヤマダ園長：

ご主人は、多くのインターナショナルスクールでは日本語の学校と同等の教科課程があることをご存じですか？基本的には子どもたちは公立学校にいるのと全く同じ日本語の内容を勉強しています。

イシカワさん：

まあ、全然知りませんでした！このことをすぐ主人に言わなくては。日本の学校に行きたくないと毎晩私たちに言うものでアヤカがかわいそうでした
彼女はとてもインターナショナルスクールに行きたがっているのです。

Q.47　Why is Ms. Ishikawa thankful to Principal Yamada?

イシカワさんはなぜヤマダ園長に感謝しているのですか？

1.　　Because he has a problem, she can help him with.

2.　　Because he supports her family.

3.　　Because he is meeting her when school isn't in session.

4.　　Because she received a gift from him.

正解　　3

解説　　3.[Because he is meeting her when school isn't in session. (放課後に会えたから)]が正解です。

Q.48　What does Ms. Ishikawa discuss with Principal Yamada?

イシカワさんはヤマダ園長と何を話しているのですか？

1.　　The differences between two schools.

2.　　The best place to study Japanese.

3.　　Reserving a school classroom.

4.　　Japanese social problems.

正解　　1

解説　　1.[The differences between two schools. (2 園の違い)] が正解です。

Q.49　　What is a good point about many international schools?

インターナショナルスクールの長所は何ですか？

1.　　　There are many students in similar situations.

2.　　　There aren't as many problems as Japanese schools.

3.　　　The students can have a bilingual curriculum.

4.　　　It is cheaper than public schools.

正解　　3

解説　　3.「The students can have a bilingual curriculum.(生徒がバイリンガル教育課程を受けられるから)」が正解です。

Q.50　　Why does Ms. Ishikawa feel sad for Ayaka?

イシカワさんなぜアヤカがかわいそうだと思うのですか？

1.　　　Because her daughter loves to speak Japanese.

2.　　　Because her husband can't speak English fluently to her.

3.　　　Because she is worried about Ayaka's sleep every night.

4.　　　Because her daughter doesn't want to attend Japanese school.

正解　　4

解説　　4.「Because her daughter doesn't want to attend Japanese school. (彼女は日本の学校に行きたくないから)」が正解です。

Section II

Listening Passage 1 Q.51-Q.55

Removing the Bubble Wrap　　「過保護にすることはやめましょう」

As parents one of the hardest things to do is finding a balance between loving and protecting our children and giving them the freedom to learn and grow. Overprotecting our children can have vastly negative consequences on child development.

As adults, we may always feel that we know what is best for our children. However, children with healthy neurological systems naturally seek out the sensory input they need on their own. You may find yourself having a natural tendency to say, "No spinning, you may get dizzy," or "Get down from that tree, you might get hurt."

However, when we restrict children from experiencing new sensations of their own free will, they may not develop the senses and motor skills necessary to take risks without getting hurt. Then we, the adults, become the barrier to healthy child development.

Children are natural risk takers. During free play, children learn to manage, control, and even overcome their fears by taking risks. Children who injured themselves by falling from heights between ages five and nine are less likely to be afraid of heights when they are eighteen years old.

On the other hand, if children never go through the process of exposing themselves to new risks, their fear can turn into a phobia. In other words, our parental anxiety can become a barrier to children's emotional development as well.

親として難しい事の一つが子どもたちを愛し守ってあげることと、自由に学び、成長することのバランスを見つけることにあります。過保護は、子どもたちの成長にとてもよくない結果をもたらすことがあります。

大人は子どもたちにとって何が一番良いのかを知っていると常に思っています。しかし、健全な精神の持ち主の子どもは自然に必要とする感覚情報を自身で探し求めます。"グルグルと回るのをやめなさい、さもないと目が回りますよ"とか"木から降りなさい、さもないとケガをしますよ"とあなたはごく普通に言っている自分に気が付くかもしれません。

しかしながら、子どもたちの自由な意志による新しい感覚的な経験を奪ってしまうと、ケガをせずに危険を冒すのに必要な判断力と運動神経が育ちません。これでは、我々大人たちが健全な子どもたちの成長の障害になってしまいます。

子どもたちは生まれつきむこうみずなのです。自由に遊びながら、子どもたちは危険を冒して恐さに対応したり、抑えたり更には打ち勝つことを学びます。5歳から9歳の時に高い所から落ちてケガをした子どもたちは１８歳になったとき高さに恐怖を覚えることがより少ないのです。

一方で、新しい危険に自分自身をさらすということが無かった子どもたちは、恐ろしさが恐怖症になることがあります。つまり、親の心配が子どもたちの感情的成長の障害にもなってしまうのです。

Letting children take risks boosts their confidence. Using a knife to whittle a stick, exploring without an adult, tending a fire, and creating a fort all have one thing in common: there is the risk of injury. Even though letting kids take risks can be scary for parents, these experiences offer considerable reward and value to growing children. When a child takes a risk, such as riding a bike for the first time, it can be frightening.

At the same time, the child is learning to overcome that fear to reach a goal. In the process of learning to ride a bike successfully, the child learns patience, perseverance, and resilience. She learns to keep trying, even when she continues to fall.

Although letting kids take risks may be scary for parents and even children at first, it is an essential part of growing up.

Taking risks allows children to overcome physical challenges and strengthens their senses at the same time. These benefits ultimately make them safer and more resilient in the long run. Risky play also allows children to overcome fears and anxiety and builds strong character.

Children need opportunities to fall and make mistakes in order to become more confident and capable when facing future life challenges.

　子どもたちに危険を冒させることは彼らの自信を高めます。棒をナイフで削ったり、大人なしで探検したり、たき火の番をしたり、砦を造ったりすることに共通項があります。それはケガをする危険があることです。子どもたちに危険を冒させることは親にとって恐いことですが、こういった経験が子どもたちの成長に沢山の褒美と価値をもたらします。子どもたちが危険を冒すとき、たとえば初めて自転車に乗る時とかはゾッとするものです。

　それと同時に子どもたちは目的を達成するために恐怖に打ち勝つことを学びます。自転車に上手く乗れるように学ぶ過程で、子どもたちは忍耐、根気強さ、強靭さを身に付けます。転び続けても、挑戦し続けることを学びます。

　子どもたちに危険を冒させることは親にとってまた、子どもたちにとっても最初は恐いことかもしれませんが成長するうえで極めて重要なことなのです。

　危険を冒すことは子どもたちが肉体的な挑戦に打ち勝ちまた、同時に精神力も強くします。このような恩恵は長い目でみれば最終的には子どもたちをより安全に、より強くします。危険な遊びはまた、子どもたちが恐怖や不安に打ち勝つことができるようになり、強い人間を作ります。

　子どもたちが将来人生の課題に向かい合う時により大きな自信と能力を身に付けるため、転び失敗する機会が必要なのです。

Q.51　What could happen if parents do not allow their children to experience new sensations?
　　　保護者が子どもたちに新しい感覚を経験させないとどうなりますか？

1.　　　The children could get hurt.

2.　　　The parents could gain motor skills.

3.　　　The children will feel uneasy.

4.　　　The parents will feel safer.

正解　　1

解説　　1.[The children could get hurt. (子どもたちがケガをするかもしれません)] が正解
　　　　です。

Q.52　Why should children be allowed to play in high places?
　　　なぜ子どもたちを高い場所で遊ばせるべきなのですか？

1.　　　They will be able to spot danger below.

2.　　　They will learn to avoid high places.

3.　　　They will overcome the fear of high places.

4.　　　They will risk falling and getting injured.

正解　　3

解説　　3.[They will overcome the fear of high places. (高いところが怖くなくなる)] が正
　　　　解です。

Q.53　What risk is NOT given as a way to boost confidence?
　　　自信をつけるために示されていない危険な手段は何ですか？

1.　　　Carving wood

2.　　　Going out without parents

3.　　　Swimming in a river

4.　　　Building a fort

正解　　3

解説　　3.[Swimming in a river(川で泳ぐ)] が正解です。

Q.54　What does risky play help children overcome?
　　　危険な遊びで子どもたちがが克服するのは何ですか？

　　　1.　　strong character
　　　2.　　challenges and strengths
　　　3.　　fear and anxiety
　　　4.　　confidcncc and capability
　　　正解　　3
　　　解説　　3.[fear and anxiety(恐怖と不安)] が正解です。

Q.55　Why is the title of this passage "Removing the Bubble Wrap" ?
　　　なぜ表題が「バブルラップ（梱包用気泡シート）の取り外し」となっているのですか？
　　　1.　　It's important for children to get injured.
　　　2.　　Children need to take risks in order to succeed.
　　　3.　　Adults need to protect children.
　　　4.　　Confidence is unnecessary for success.
　　　正解　　2
　　　解説　　バブルラップ（梱包用気泡シート）はものを保護するものなので、ここでは
　　　　　　2.[Children need to take risks in order to succeed.（子どもたちは成功のためには
　　　　　　リスクをとることが必要（過保護になりすぎないを例えて表現している）] が正解
　　　　　　です。

 Section II

Listening Passage 2 Q.56-Q.60

Doing homework can be a stressful activity for parents and children alike. Most of the time, children put off finishing their homework because they think it's a tiresome task that will take them hours to finish. Kids naturally want to have fun and will choose playing games over doing tedious assignments any day.

宿題をするというのは、親にとっても子どもたちにとっても同様にストレスがかかるものです。
宿題を終えるまで何時間もかかる面倒な作業と思いだいたい子どもたちは先延ばしにします
子どもたちは当然楽しいことをしたいと思っているので、いつでもうんざりする宿題をするよりもゲームで遊ぶことを選びます。

Many things compete for their attention, from TV shows and video games to mobile phones and the Internet.

テレビ、ビデオゲームから携帯電話、インターネットまで彼らにはたくさんの誘惑があります。

As a parent, your role is crucial in shaping your child's study and homework habits. You want your child to develop good study habits and to do their homework diligently. However, constantly punishing, nagging, or arguing with your child rarely works for the long term, and such methods only cause more resistance, whining, and complaints.

子どもたちの勉強や宿題を習慣づける上で、親としてのあなたの役割は重要です。あなたは子どもたちに勉強の習慣を身につけ、宿題を真面目にして欲しいのです。しかしながら、子どもたちに対してたえず罰したり、小言を言ったり、言い争うのは長い目でみて何の効果もありませんし、そのようなやり方では、さらなる反抗、不平不満、文句のもとになるだけです。

The following steps can help you to set up a homework routine and that will encourage your child to complete their assignments happily each day.

以下の方法は宿題を習慣づけ、子どもたちが宿題を毎日楽しく終えるように仕向けます。

Step 1: Establish a homework routine on the first day of school.

Creating a regular homework routine that involves when and where assignments should be done is essential. Students greatly benefit from clear structures for completing homework. It's often easier to accomplish tasks when they are tied to certain routines.

方法１：学校初日に、宿題を日課にすることを決める。
いつ、どこで宿題をするかを含めた規則的な日課を作り上げることが重要です。生徒は宿題を終える明確な方法に多いに助けられます。日課にすることで多くはより簡単に達成できます。

Step 2: Find a suitable space in your home where your child can do homework.

The right location depends on your child's preferences. Some kids find it comfortable to work in their rooms, where the quiet ambiance promotes concentration. Others are easily distracted by playthings in their bedroom, so are likely to perform better at a location with fewer distractions, such as the dining room table.

Ask your child about where they'll feel most relaxed. Ideally, the location should be quiet, clean, and free of distraction, allowing your child to stay focused.

Step 3: Create a homework center.

After identifying the location most conducive to completing homework, the next step is to set it up as a homework center. Ensure that the workspace is roomy enough to accommodate all necessary materials for doing assignments. Find out the types of supplies your child typically uses, and provide all basic supplies, including pencils, pens, papers, colored markers, and rulers. A dictionary, thesaurus, and calculator may also be necessary.

Step 4: Choose a homework time.

It's essential to establish a particular time for doing homework every day. Your child should be able to get used to this schedule until it becomes a normal daily routine. It's also good to do homework after dinner when children feel full and their energy levels have been replenished.

方法２：家の中で子どもたちが宿題をする適切な場所を見つける。

最適な場所は子どもの好みによります。ある子どもは自分の部屋が心地良いと感じ、静かな状況が集中力を高めてくれます。ある子どもたちは自分の寝室にあるおもちゃに容易に気が散らされるので、おもちゃがほとんど置かれていない食卓テーブルなどが良い場所に思われます。

あなたの子どもに最も落ち着くできる場所を聞いてみてください。理想を言えば、子どもが集中できる静かで清潔で気が散らない場所が良いでしょう。

方法３：宿題センターをつくる。

宿題を終えるのに最適の場所が分かったら、次はそこを宿題センターに決めることです。

そこが宿題をするに必要な道具をすべて置くことができる十分な広さがあることを確認してください。子どもがよく使う必需品を探し、全ての必要最低限の文房具、例えば鉛筆、ペン、紙、色マーカー、定規などを準備しましょう。辞書、百科辞典、計算機も必要かもしれません。

方法４：宿題時間を決める。

毎日宿題をする時間を決めることが大切です。通常の日課になるまで、子どもはこの予定に慣れることが必要です。また、子どもたちが満腹で、活力レベルが最高の夕食後に宿題をすることもいいでしょう。

However, avoid doing assignments later in the evening, because your child may feel too exhausted to think. **Step 5: Include breaks.** Working on assignments continuously can quickly drain your child physically and mentally. Let him decide when he'd like to take a break, and include his chosen break periods in the daily homework schedule. **Step 6: Offer rewards.** Mark your homework calendar for each day of successful completion of assignments, and offer rewards and incentives on certain days. Access to electronics, playtime with friends, or the purchase of new video game at the end of the month are all great incentives.	ただ、あまり夜遅くに宿題をするのは、子どもは考えることに疲れすぎてしまうかもしれないので避けたほうがよいでしょう。 **方法5：休憩を入れる。** 宿題をし続けることは、肉体的にも精神的にも子どもを速く消耗させます。子どもにいつ休憩をとりたいか決めさせ、日々の宿題予定表に選んだ休憩時間を入れましょう。 **手順6：ご褒美をあげる。** 宿題を終えることができた日を宿題予定表にマークしましょう。そして一定の日数にご褒美や励みとなるものを与えましょう。電子機器をさせたり、友達と遊ぶ時間をつくったり、月末に新しいビデオゲームの購入など、全てがとても励みとなるものです。

Q.56　　What is NOT one of the things mentioned that distracts children from homework?
　　　　宿題から子どもたちの気を散らすことについて述べられていないことは何ですか？

1.　　　TV
2.　　　Games
3.　　　Tiresome tasks
4.　　　Internet

正解　　3

解説　　3.[Tiresome tasks（疲れる作業）] が正解です。

Section II

Q.57　According to the speaker, what should parents do on the first day of school?

話者によれば登校初日に保護者がするべきことは何ですか？

1.　　　Allow children to play to get rid of stress.

2.　　　Do the homework for their children.

3.　　　Discuss the school day with their children.

4.　　　Start a daily schedule for doing homework.

正解　　4

解説　　4.[Start a daily schedule for doing homework.［（宿題の毎日の計画の開始）］が正解です。

Q.58　Where is a good place for children to study at home?

家で勉強する良い場所は？

1.　　　In the bedroom

2.　　　In the dining room

3.　　　At the library

4.　　　At the parent's workplace

正解　　2

解説　　2.[In the dining room（ダイニングルーム）] が正解です。

Q.59　Why is it a good idea to do homework after dinner?

夕食後に宿題をするのはなぜ良い考えなのですか？

1.　　　Because the children will have more energy.

2.　　　Because they should help with dinner.

3.　　　Because they will feel tired at this time.

4.　　　Because they have homework everyday.

正解　　1

解説　　1.[Because the children will have more energy.（子たちにもっとエネルギーがあるから）] が正解です。

Section II

Q.60　What would be the best title for this passage?
　　　このパッセージに最も適切なタイトルは何だと思いますか？

1.　　Homework Makes Us Happy

2.　　Too Much Homework is Stressful

3.　　Designing a Homework Routine

4.　　Avoiding Homework is Important

正解　　3

解説　　3.[Designing a Homework Routine (宿題の習慣をデザイン、工夫する)] が正解です。

Listening Passage 3 Q.61-Q.66

A Description of IB Curriculum Programs　　IB教育課程プログラムについて

The International Baccalaureate Program, or IB Program for short was founded in Geneva, Switzerland in 1968 where it is also headquartered. The IB offers programming for Primary, Middle School, and High School levels. In order to host these programs, schools must go through a rigorous accreditation process where the IB organization will evaluate everything from school facilities, health and sanitation, to teacher training and effectiveness.	国際バカロレア・プログラム (略称 IB) は 1968 年にスイス、ジュネーブで設立され、ここが本部にもなっています。IB は小学校、中学校、高等学校レベル向けのプログラムを提供します。これらプログラムを受けるためには、学校は厳しい認定プロセスを経なければなりません。IB は学校の設備、健康衛生設備から先生の養成、実効性まで審査します。
The IB curriculum is the world's first curriculum designed specifically for the international context and international schools. The IB curriculum values diversity, global mindeness, and diplomacy. The IB approach is completely different from traditional educational methods. There are no examinations, but instead students are assessed on their ability to apply their knowledge in realistic and practical ways.	IB 教育課程は特に国際分野および国際学校（インターナショナルスクール）向けに作られた世界で初めての教育課程で、多様性、国際感覚性、外交性を重んじます。IB の取り組み方は、従来の教育方法とは全く異なります。試験はありませんが、代わりに生徒は現実的で実用的な方法で彼らの知識を応用する能力で評価されます。

Throughout the year students develop a portfolio of their work that can contain projects, experiments, and community work on which they will be assessed. The IB diploma is highly recognized and coveted by universities around the globe due to its rigor and practical application towards both university study and real life situations.

年間を通し生徒は研究課題、実地経験、社会活動を含む成果について評価ツールをつくりあげ、これらが評価されるのです。IB修了証書は、その厳しさと、大学での研究や実生活の状況に実用的に応用できることから世界中の大学で高く評価され熱望されています。

Q.61　What age levels does the IB Program provide services for?

IB プログラムはどの年齢層に提供していますか？

1.　　Ages 0 - 12

2.　　Ages 0 - 18

3.　　Ages 5 - 18

4.　　Ages 12 - 20

正解　　3

解説　　内容から3.［Ages 5 – 18（5 – 18 歳）］が正解です。

Q.62　What does the IB organization check when visiting a school?

国際バカロレア機構は学校訪問時何を調べますか？

1.　　The quality of students

2.　　The grading process

3.　　The training of students

4.　　The school building

正解　　4

解説　　4.［The school building.（学校設備）］が正解です。

Section II

Q.63　How are students graded under the IB Program?

　　　IB プログラムでは、学生はどのように成績がつけられますか？

　　　1.　　By rigorous tests

　　　2.　　Through realistic processes

　　　3.　　The community grades them

　　　4.　　Through the local university

　　　正解　　2

　　　解説　　2.［Through realistic processes.(現実的プロセス)］が正解です。

Q.64　What was the IB curriculum designed to accomplish?

　　　IB カリキュラムは何を達成するためにつくられましたか？

　　　1.　　like-mindedness

　　　2.　　traditional values

　　　3.　　a variety of thought

　　　4.　　better English skills

　　　正解　　3

　　　解説　　3.［a variety of thought(多様な考え方)］が正解です。

Q.65　What do the students create during the year?

　　　生徒たちは年間を通して何を創作しますか？

　　　1.　　A collection of all the work and projects they've done.

　　　2.　　A global network of connections for work.

　　　3.　　A portfolio of all their examinations.

　　　4.　　A university application.

　　　正解　　1

　　　解説　　1.［A collection of all the work and projects they've done.（彼らが行ったすべての
　　　　　　作業とプロジェクトの集大成）］が正解です。

Q.66　　　What is the benefit of graduating from the IB Program?

IB プログラムを卒業することの利点は何ですか？

1.　　　　You can travel to Switzerland.

2.　　　　You can gain real-life experience.

3.　　　　It's equivalent to a university degree.

4.　　　　It has great examinations.

正解　　　2

解説　　　2.［You can gain real-life experience.（生きた人生経験を積むことができます）］が
正解です。

第3回　問題

解答解説

Level Pre-1 第3回　解答

Q.1	4
Q.2	2
Q.3	1
Q.4	2
Q.5	4
Q.6	3
Q.7	1
Q.8	2
Q.9	4
Q.10	2
Q.11	2
Q.12	4
Q.13	2
Q.14	1
Q.15	1
Q.16	2
Q.17	4
Q.18	1
Q.19	2
Q.20	2

Q.21	2
Q.22	3
Q.23	1
Q.24	4
Q.25	4
Q.26	1
Q.27	3
Q.28	3
Q.29	1
Q.30	4
Q.31	3
Q.32	4
Q.33	1
Q.34	3
Q.35	4
Q.36	3
Q.37	1
Q.38	2
Q.39	4
Q.40	3

Q.42	3
Q.43	2
Q.44	3
Q.45	2
Q.46	1
Q.47	2
Q.48	1
Q.49	4
Q.50	2
Q.51	4
Q.52	2
Q.53	1
Q.54	3
Q.55	4
Q.56	4
Q.57	4
Q.58	1
Q.59	2
Q.60	4
Q.61	2
Q62	3
Q.63	4
Q.64	1
Q.65	3
Q.66	4

Q.41

Ms. Suzuki and Ms.Yamanaka talked about the weekend. Ms. Suzuki went to an amusement park with her boyfriend and rode many rides. Unfortunately, the roller coaster was closed for repairs.

 Section I

Q.1　正解　4　　　a total of

解説　[タロウは今朝 3 回嘔吐しました] という内容ですから、4. の [a total of(合計)] が正解です。1.[a sum of] も合計ですが、算数や金額の合計といった場合に使用します。2. [a quotient of (割り算の商)]、3.[a portion(部分)] という意味です。

Q.2　正解　2　　　sign up

解説　[リエ、もうバレー教室の申込みはしましたか] という内容ですから、2.[sign up(申し込む、登録する)] が正解です。

Q.3　正解　1　　　buckle

解説　[みなさん、安全のためシートベルトを締めてくださいね] という内容ですから、1.[buckle(バックル・締め金で留める)] が正解です。2.[mend] は [直す、繕う]、3.[unhook] は [ホックを外す]、4.[disengage] は [解放する] という意味です。

Q.4　正解　2　　　concerned

解説　[タロウの体調がちょっと心配です。彼は数日食べていません] という内容ですから、2.[concerned(心配する)] が正解です。

Q.5　正解　4　　　flooded

解説　[昨夜は大雨だったので、すべての道が水没しました] という内容ですから、4.[flooded(水浸しの)] が正解です。3.[humidity] は [湿気] です。

Q.6　正解　3　　　difficult

解説　[今朝のタロウは言うことを聞かなくて洋服を着たがりません] という内容ですから、3.[difficult(言うことを聞かなくて困る、難しい、面倒な)] が正解です。

Q.7　正解　1　　　come true

解説　[お願いをすれば、いつかそれは叶うでしょう] という内容ですから、1.[come true(叶う)] が正解です。

Q.8　　正解　　2　　　afraid that

解説　　「タロウは病気なので残念ですがパーティーに来られないと思う」という内容です
　　　　から、2.[afraid that(残念だが～と思う)] が正解です。

Q.9　　What does the expression "first come first serve" mean?

「先着順」という表現の意味は何ですか？

1.　　that people who arrive early must help assist others

2.　　that arriving early improves your performance

3.　　that everyone must arrive in the order they are scheduled

4.　　that people are served in the order that they arrive

正解　　4　　　　　that people are served in the order that they arrive

解説　　4.[that people are served in the order that they arrive(到着順に対応される)] が正
　　　　解です。

Q.10　　What does it mean to be "keen"？

「熱心な」と言う意味は何ですか？

1.　　to be sly

2.　　to like something or be interested in doing it

3.　　to be intelligent and charming

4.　　to oppose an activity or suggestion

正解　　2　　　　　to like something or be interested in doing it

解説　　2. [to like something or be interested in doing it(何かを好きになったり、何かをす
　　　　ることに興味を持ったりする)] が適切です。

Section II

Dialogue 1 Q.11-Q.20　保護者二人の会話

Mariko:	こんにちは、ジュディさん!運動会のプログラムは受け取った?
Judy:	受け取ったわ。今年の予定種目にはびっくりだわ!
Mariko:	コトネが綱引きをすごく楽しみにしているのよ!
Judy:	ねぇ、親が子どもと一緒に参加出来るか知ってる?
Mariko:	知ってるわよ!家族は、ほとんど一緒に参加出来るのよ。
Judy:	すごい!すごくいいニュースだわ!
Mariko:	当日お天気はどうなるのか知ってる?
Judy:	今のところ、予報は、晴れて暑くなるらしいわよ。
Mariko:	じゃ、子どもたちに日焼け止めを沢山詰めていくようにするわ。

Q.11　　正解　　2　　　　program
　　　　解説　　[運動会のプログラムを受け取りましたか] という内容ですから、2.[program] が正解です。

Q.12　　正解　　4　　　　events
　　　　解説　　[今年の予定種目は〜] という内容ですから4.[events(種目)]が正解です。

Q.13　　正解　　2　　　　participate
　　　　解説　　[親も子どもと一緒に参加出来る] という内容ですから、2.[participate(参加する)] が正解です。4.[foreit] は [代償、罰金] という意味です。

Q.14　　正解　　1　　　　absolutely
　　　　解説　　[すごくいいニュースだわ] と言っているので、1.[absolutely(完全に、断然)] という意味があるので正解です。3.[dubiously] は [疑っている]、4. [questionably] は [疑問の余地がある] いう意味です。

Q.15　　正解　　1　　　　pack
　　　　解説　　[沢山の日焼け止めを詰めていく」という内容ですから、1.[pack(詰める、詰めて持っていく)] が正解です。2.[bundle] は名詞では [束] ですが、動詞では [立ち去る]、4.[bunch] は [束ねる] という意味です。

Section II

Dialogue 2　Q.16-Q.20 保護者と園長の会話

保護者：　こんにちは！年末の子ども達の発表会のご支援をしていただけないかと思いまして。

園長：　　もちろんです！喜んで支援いたします。

保護者：　ありがとうございます！子ども達皆がそれぞれ違う動物の衣裳の調整を手伝って頂きたいのですが。

園長：　　いいですよ！リハーサルの前までにすべての衣裳の準備が出来るようにします。

保護者：　ありがとうございます！公式練習を始める前に用意出来るのはすばらしいです。

園長：　　私にお任せください！すぐ準備を始めます。

Q.16　　正解　　2　　　　performance
　　　　解説　　［子ども達の発表会の支援］という内容ですから、2.[performance(発表会)]が正解です。

Q.17　　正解　　4　　　　help out
　　　　解説　　「喜んでお手伝いします」と言っていますから、4.[help out(助ける、手伝う)]が正解です。

Q.18　　正解　　1　　　　costumes
　　　　解説　　［子どもたちの衣裳の調整を手伝って頂きたい」という内容ですから、1.[costume(衣裳)]が正解です。

Q.19　　正解　　2　　　　prior
　　　　解説　　「リハーサルの前に衣裳を用意する」という内容ですから、2.[prior to(先立って、～より前に)]が正解です。

Q.20　　正解　　2　　　　count
　　　　解説　　「お任せください」という意味ですから、2.[count on me]が正解です。

Section III

Reading Passage 1　Q.21- Q.35

幼児教育は人生の成功の鍵です

"早ければ早い程よい" は幼児教育の的確なスローガンです。個人的にまた、経歴という点において
も生涯の自己達成感を保証する特効薬はありません。しかし、徹底した調査によれば質の高い幼児
教育は学校や職場また社会領域において継続的な成功を促進する一つの非常に強力な手段でありま
す。

意外かもしれませんが、幼児期の経験は学校やそれ以降に経験することに較べて、とても大きな効
果があります。この時期に遅れがでてしまうと、取り返す機会がないでしょう。学習しながら弱点
部分の強化を試みることは、早い時期に学習するよりはるかに難しく費用もかかります。良いことは、
幼児に焦点を当てた高等プログラムは、どのような環境で育った子どもたちにも強力で長期的な効
果があることです。

最近の調査が示すところでは、質の高い幼稚園に通った子どもたちの多くは高校や大学を卒業する
だけでなく、就職直後から多くの収入を得る傾向にあるようです。またこれらの子どもの多くは親
になり家庭を持ち、麻薬や薬物乱用で問題になる可能性はより低くなります。また、長期的な調査
ではこれらの子どもは将来犯罪で逮捕される可能性も低くなるということです。

本調査は、全ての大人が質の高い幼児教育を経てスタートを切れば、社会全体が恩恵を受けること
を示しています。国の福祉支援を必要とする人は減り、犯罪率は下がり、総じて住民はより健康的
になります。また、社会はより多くの熟練労働力の恩恵を受けます。

質の高い幼児教育は受けた人が学校の内外で生涯にわたり間違いなく成功することを保証する特効
薬ではありません。多くの他の要因が影響しますが子どもたちの質の高い初期教育の社会的および
経済的恩恵は共に充実したものでまた継続するという圧倒的な証拠があります。参加する子どもが
恩恵を受けるだけでなく、また我々社会も総じて恩恵を受けるのです。

Q.21-Q.24

　　　正解　　Q.21　2 perfect　　　Q.22　3 lifetime　　　Q.23　1 research　　　Q.24　4 promote

　　　解説　　Q.21　2.[perfect] は [正確な、完全な] という意味です。Q.22　自己達成の [一生] を保証することで3.[lifetime] が正解です。Q.23　[調査] ということで1.[research] が正解です。Q.24　継続的な成功を [促進する] の意味がある 4.[promote] が正解です。

Q.25-Q.29

　　　正解　　Q.25　4 It may seem　　　Q.26　1 in comparison　　　Q.27　3 catch up

　　　　　　　Q.28　3 focused on　　　Q.29　1 showed that

　　　解説　　Q.25　4.[It may seem surprising(意外かもしれないが)] という意味になるので、4 が正解です。1.[It may become] は [それはなるかもしれません]、2.[It doesn't] は、[それはしません]、3.[Some might say] は [あるものは言うかもしれない] 問う意味です。

　　　　　　　Q.26　前段と後段の経験を比較することですから1.[in comparison (比較して)] が正解です。2.[in retrospect] は [振り返ってみると]、3.[in hindsight] は [後知恵で、後から振り返って]、4.[in correlation] は [相関関係にある] という意味です。

　　　　　　　Q.27　3.[catch up(追いつく)] が正解です。

　　　　　　　Q.28　3.[focused on(焦点を当てる)] が正解です。

　　　　　　　Q.29　[最近の調査が示す] という内容ですから、1.[showed that(示している)] が正解です。

Q.30　　正解　　4

　　　　解説　　麻薬、薬物につながる 4.[abuse(乱用)] が正解です。

Q.31　　正解　　3

　　　　解説　　段落 3 と 4 によると、質の高い幼児教育の恩恵としてあげられてないのは以下の中でどれですか？という設問です。

　　　　　　　　3.[Decreased rates of mental retardation（知的障害減少率）] に関しては述べていませんので3. が正解です。

Q.32　　正解　　4

解説　　段落5にある”magic bullet”と言う語句の意味はなんですか？という設問です。
[magic bullet(特効薬)]と同じ意味の4.[A fool proof solution(絶対確実の解決策)]が正解です。

Q.33　　正解　　1

解説　　段落5 overwhelming(圧倒的)の同義語は何ですか？との設問です。1.[staggering]が正解です。

Q.34　　正解　　3

解説　　3.[this benefits not just the children.(これは子どものためになるだけではない)]が正解です。

Q.35　　正解　　4

解説　　パッセージの内容から質の高い幼児教育で第一に恩恵を受けるのは何ですか？)」という設問です。4.[all children.(全ての子どもたち)]が正解です。

Reading Passage 2 Q.36-Q.40
キッズ・パティオ幼稚園から夏季慈善イベント企画についての手紙

> キッズ・パティオ保護者各位
>
> キッズ・パティオ幼稚園はまた今年も夏季慈善イベントを開催いたします。昨年の赤十字基金との企画は大成功でしたので、今年もイベントを行うことにしました。今年はスポンサー付きの“ミニ・マラソン”を行います。子どもたちはスポンサーシートを受け取り、慈善レースに参加し、お金を寄付して頂けるスポンサーを見つけゴールします。レースの長さは次ぎの通りです。
>
> 　　　　　3歳半以下の子ども　　　　500 m
> 　　　　　3歳半以上の子ども　　　1000 m
> このイベントは通常の登園日に行いますので、保護者の方には公開いたしません。梅雨の時期ということもあり開催予定日は、仮とし柔軟に対応できるようにするためです。また、4 Ocean 慈善事業と一緒に行います。この4 Ocean 慈善事業は世界の海や海岸線からプラスティックやゴミの除去を促進するもので、数えきれない数の海洋生物を救うだけでなく、我々の地球の美しさを保つことにもなり、とても価値ある取り組みです。

> スポンサー用紙は本日、子どもたちのバックパックに入れて持ち帰ります。この大切な活動についてお子様たちと話し合い、6月8日金曜日までに全ての後援者と寄付金をお子さまの名前を書いた封筒に入れて戻してください。ご質問がある場合は、お子さんの担当の先生にお話しください。ご協力ありがとうございます。
>
> 　　　　　　　　　　　　　　　　　　　　　　　　　　　　　　　　ヤマダ園長

Q.36-Q.38
　　　　文章中の（Q.36）、（Q.37）,（Q.38）にあてはまる一語を下記リストから選びなさい。
　　　　一語はどれにもあてはまりません。

　　　　1. flexible　　　　　　2. preserve　　　　　　3. successful　　　　　4. collaborate

　　　　正解　Q.36：3　　Q.37：1　　Q.38：2

　　　　解説　　Q.36　　　昨年のイベントが 3.[successful(成功)] だったが正解です。

　　　　　　　　Q.37　　　文中の [remain tentative] を補足する 1.[flexible(柔軟な、融通の効く)]が正解です。

　　　　　　　　Q.38　　　（地球の美しさ）を 2.[preserve(維持する)] が正解です。

Q.39　　　お知らせによると保護者はこのイベントのためにいつ到着するべきかと述べていますか？

　　　　1.　　　　On Friday, June 8th.

　　　　2.　　　　Only after their child has found a sponsor.

　　　　3.　　　　After the rainy season.

　　　　4.　　　　Parents are not allowed to attend.

　　　　正解　　4

　　　　解説　　文中で (保護者には公開されません) とあるので 4.[Parents are not allowed to attend(保護者は参加は出できない)] が正解です。

Q.40　　　お知らせによるとこのチャリティ行事の慈善興行にならないのは以下の中でどれですか？

　　　　1. Saving marine wildlife.

　　　　2. Removing trash from the ocean.

　　　　3. Taking a trip to the beach.

　　　　4. Protecting the beauty of our planet.

　　　　正解　　3

　　　　解説　　3.[海岸に出かける] は本文では触れられていないので正解です。

 Section IV

Writing

スズキさん：	ヤマナカさん、この週末は何をしたの？
ヤマナカさん：	土曜の朝にボーイフレンドと遊園地に行ったの！
スズキさん：	うわぁ、それは楽しそうね。どうだった？
ヤマナカさん：	開園時間の8時ちょうどに着いたから沢山の乗り物に乗れたのよ！
スズキさん：	それはよかった。私の好きな乗り物はローラーコースターよ。
ヤマナカさん：	私も。。。でも残念ながら修理中で閉まっていたの。来月、再開するけどね。

Q.41　　　対話を読んで対話の内容を30ワードでまとめなさい。

採点基準

1. Writing 専用の用紙に記入すること

2. 鈴木さんとヤマナカさんの対話の内容が正しく説明されていること

3. 文法、スペリング、字数が正確であること

＊字数にカンマ、ピリオドは含みません。

正解例：　　Ms. Suzuki and Ms. Yamanaka talked about the weekend. Ms. Suzuki went to an amusement park with her boyfriend and rode many rides. Unfortunately, the roller coaster was closed for repairs.

第3回　問題

リスニング問題　解説（放送問題付き）

 Section I

Dialogue 1　インターン学生と園長の対話

Principal Yamada: Good morning, Ms. Yamaguchi. I have called this meeting this　morning because we are concerned about your performance in the internship program.	**ヤマダ園長：** おはようございます、ヤマグチさん。面談に今朝あなたを呼んだのは、あなたのインターンシップ・プログラムでの行動を私たちが皆で、懸念しているからです。
Ms. Yamaguchi: Okay, can you tell me what I am doing wrong?	**ヤマグチさん：** そうですか、私の何が悪いのか教えて頂けますか？
Principal Yamada: First of all, you already have three unexcused late arrivals during your first two weeks. Punctuality is essential for all teaching is professionals.	**ヤマダ園長：** 先ず、最初の2週間で正当な理由のない遅刻を既に3回もあります。時間を守るということは、教師という職業には絶対必要なことです。
Ms. Yamaguchi: I know, I'm sorry. It's just that sometimes it takes a long time to make my bento in the morning and I end up missing my train.	**ヤマグチさん：** わかっています、申し訳ありません。ただ、時々、朝お弁当を作るのに時間がかかってしまい、結果、電車に乗り遅れてしまうのです。
Principal Yamada: Ms. Yamaguchi…I'm sorry to say, but that's not a good enough reason. We all have to make lunch and get to work. You're not the only one who has to do these things. Comments like that could make your co-workers lose faith in you as a teammate.	**ヤマダ園長：** ヤマグチさん、、、言いたくはないのですが、それは理由にはなりません。皆、お弁当をつくって仕事にくるのです。あなただけがこれらをやっているわけではないのですよ。そのような言い訳はチームメイトとして同僚の信頼をなくしかねますよ。

Ms. Yamaguchi:	ヤマグチさん：
You are completely right. The truth is I have just gotten so used to being a lazy college student, that this sample of real life has been a bit overwhelming. I see I have a lot of growing to do.	おっしゃる通りです。本当の事を言えば、ただ怠けた学生に慣れすぎていました。このような現実の生活は、少しつらかったです。自分が成長しなければならない事が沢山あるとわかります。
Principal Yamada:	ヤマダ園長：
I'm glad you see that and that you are learning this lesson. It will help you be more prepared to succeed. With that being said, please understand that any further unexcused late arrivals will result in the early termination of your internship.	わかってくれて嬉しいし、あなたがこの教訓から学んでくれることも嬉しいことです。あなたが成功するための心構えを身につけることにも役立ちます。とは言え、今後正当な理由のない遅刻をした場合は、インターンシップが早期終了になることを承知しておくように。

Q.42　　Why did Principal Yamada want to meet with Ms. Yamaguchi?
　　　　なぜ、ヤマダ園長はヤマグチさんに会いたかったのですか？

　　1.　　To discuss her trial teaching lesson.
　　2.　　To give her advice about the teaching profession.
　　3.　　To discuss issues with her performance in the internship program.
　　4.　　To fire her from Kids Patio.

　　正解　　3

　　解説　　対話より、3.[To give her advice about the teaching profession.（インターンシップ・プログラムで彼女の行動上の問題点を話すため）] が正解です。

Q.43　　What was Principal Yamada's main issue with Ms. Yamaguchi？
　　　　ヤマダ園長のヤマグチさんに対する主な問題は何ですか？

　　　　1.　　　She had been acting rudely towards co-workers.

　　　　2.　　　She arrived late several times.

　　　　3.　　　She had been quite lazy.

　　　　4.　　　She took too many days off work.

　　　　正解　　2

　　　　解説　　対話より、2.[She arrived late several times.(彼女は数回遅刻しました)]が正解です。

Q.44　　What was Ms. Yamaguchi's first excuse for her behavior?
　　　　自分の態度についてヤマグチさんの最初のいい訳は何でしたか？

　　　　1.　　　She is a lazy college student.

　　　　2.　　　She wasn't aware of school policy.

　　　　3.　　　She had to make her lunch.

　　　　4.　　　She was influenced by other teachers.

　　　　正解　　3

　　　　解説　　対話より 3.[She had to make her lunch.(お弁当を作らなければならなかった)] が
　　　　　　　正解です。

Q.45　　Why do you think Ms. Yamaguchi is struggling with her role?
　　　　ヤマグチさんは自分の務めになぜ苦労していると思いますか？

　　　　1.　　　She is an unskilled teacher.

　　　　2.　　　She is overwhelmed by professional life.

　　　　3.　　　She is getting poor guidance from other teachers.

　　　　4.　　　She lacks knowledge of school rules and policies.

　　　　正解　　2

　　　　解説　　対話より 2.[She is overwhelmed by professional life.(職業生活にいっぱいいっぱい
　　　　　　　の状態です)] が正解です。

Section I

Q.46　What will happen if Ms. Yamaguchi's poor performance continues?
ヤマグチさんのふさわしくない行動が続くとどうなりますか？

1.　Principal Yamada will terminate her internship.

2.　Principal Yamada will give her an official letter of warning.

3.　Principal Yamada will assign her a new mentor.

4.　Principal Yamada will personally mentor her.

正解　　1

解説　　1.[Principal Yamada will terminate her internship.（ヤマダ園長は彼女のインターンシップを終らせる。）] が正解です。

Dialogue 2　保護者とヤマダ園長の対話

Mrs. Iwamoto:	イワモトさん：
Principal Yamada thank you for meeting me on short notice. I am here to discuss one of your teachers, Mr. Ito. Yesterday afternoon during afternoon clean up time I heard Mr. Ito screaming at one of the children. He sounded so angry.	急にもかかわらずお会い頂きましてありがとうございます。先生の1人のイトウ先生についてご相談したく参りました。昨日、午後の清掃時間の時に、イトウ先生が子どもの1人に叫んでいるのを聞きました。とても怒っているようでした。
Principal Yamada:	ヤマダ園長：
Thank you for coming to speak with me, Ms. Iwamoto. I am aware of the incident and am very disappointed. You have my apologies.	イワモトさん、お話しにいらしてくだりありがとうございます。私もその件は知っており、とてもがっかりしています。申し訳ございません。
Mrs. Iwamoto:	イワモトさん：
Please know that Mr. Ito has a negative reputation amongst parents. My family just doesn't feel comfortable with him on staff, so we are here to officially cancel our enrollment.	知っておいて頂きたいのですが、保護者の間ではイトウ先生の評判は良くないのです。私の家族も彼が職員でいることを良く思っておりませんので、正式に入園の取り消しに参りました。

Principal Yamada:	ヤマダ園長：
I am so sad to hear that. We truly love having Ritsu and Koiya in the Kids Patio family. We are currently working to replace Mr. Ito. Mr. Takagi will be taking over his class from the first of next month.	それは残念なことです。リツとコイヤがキッズ・パティオ園の一員になって頂きたいと思っています。現在、イトウ先生を交替するよう動いています。来月最初からタカギ先生がイトウ先生のクラスを引き継ぐ予定です。
Mrs. Iwamoto:	イワモトさん：
I am sure many families will be releived. Unfortunately, I have already enrolled Ritsu and Koiya in a new school.	多くの家族がホットすること間違いなしです。でも残念ですが、既にリツとコイヤは新しい園に入学申込済みです。
Principal Yamada:	ヤマダ園長：
I completely understand. We will certainly miss you and are happy to welcome you back anytime.	よくわかりました。とても残念ですがいつでも戻ってきてくださいね。
Mrs. Iwamato:	イワモトさん：
Thank you, Principal Yamada. I wish I had spoken to you sooner. The kids absolutely love it here and truthfully, they do not want to change schools. Who knows maybe we will be back one day.	ヤマダ園長先生、ありがとうございます。もっと早くお話しすればよかったです。子どもたちはとてもこの園が好きで、本当は学校を変えたいなんて思っていません。いつかまた戻ってお世話になるかもしれません。。

Q.47　　　It's clear from the passage that the meeting was...
　　　　　内容から、面談は・・・が明らかです。

1.　　　scheduled a long time ago
2.　　　scheduled on short notice
3.　　　spontaneous
4.　　　after school hours

　　　　正解　　　2

　　　　解説　　　対話の内容から [on short notice] と言っているので 2.[scheduled on short notice(直前の通知で予定された)] が正解です。

Q.48　What is Mrs. Iwamoto's issue?

イワモトさんの問題は何ですか？

1.　That Mr. Ito yelled at the children in anger.

2.　That Mr. Ito is an unskilled teacher.

3.　That Mr. Takagi screamed at the children.

4.　That Mr. Takagi is often late.

正解　　1

解説　　対話から 1.[That Mr. Ito yelled at the children in anger.（イトウ先生が、怒りなが
ら怒鳴った）] が正解です。

Q.49　It is clear from the dialogue that the problem teacher...

対話の内容から明らかなのは、問題の教師は、、、

1.　had received a written warning from Principal Yamada

2.　had cases of physical issue abuse

3.　got along very poorly with his co-teachers

4.　has a negative reputation amongst the parents

正解　　4

解説　　4.[has a negative reputation amongst the parents（保護者の間で評判が悪い）] が」
が正解です。

Q.50　What was Mrs. Iwamoto's final decision?

イワモトさんの最終決断は何ですか？

1.　To keep her children out of school until there is a teacher change.

2.　To enroll her children in a new school.

3.　To change to a new class in Kids Patio within the same level.

4.　To wait and allow Principal Yamada to handle the situation.

正解　　2

解説　　2.[To enroll her children in a new school.（彼女の子どもたちを新しい園に入学させ
る）] が正解です。

Section II

Listening Passage 1　Q.51-Q.55
オープンハウスについてヤマダ園長からキッズ・パティオ園の保護者へのメッセージ

Dear Kids Patio Families,

　We are writing to inform you that Open House signups are now available. Open House will be held at Kids Patio from September 4th – 8th.

　Open House is a week-long event, held twice yearly, where parents are able to sign up to come and observe their child's normal school day and classes.

　Open House at Kids Patio is designed to provide parents with a greater insight into their child's life and development.

　While at the Open House feel free to involve yourself in your child's activities and do be aware that the presence of many families during the school day will change their behavior. Some children may act unusually shy, while others may cry out of anxiety due to wondering what all the changes are about. Nevertheless, we hope that you will be able to walk away from the Open House feeling a sense of pride in your children.

　The signup sheet is located at the school entrance. Please be sure to sign up for the specific dates, times, and levels that you would like to attend. Each family is allowed to visit one day only. Signups for Open House will officially close on Friday, September 1st. Late sign-ups are unavailable. Thank you for your cooperation.

　　　　　　　Sincerely,
　　　　　　　Principal Yamada

キッズ・パティオ園保護者各位

　オープンハウス参加への申し込みが可能になりました。オープンハウスは9月4日〜8日の間キッズ・パティオ園で行います。

　オープンハウスは1週間にわたるイベントで年2回行なわれ保護者にはお申し込みの上、子どもたちの日常の園生活や授業の様子を参観していただけます。

　キッズ・パティオ園のオープンハウスは保護者の皆様に子どもたちの生活、成長について一定のご理解をいただけるような機会となればと考えております。

　オープンハウス中は、お子様たちの活動に自由にご参加ください。多くのご家族がいらっしゃることで子どもたちの態度にも変化が起きますのでそちらも合わせてご覧ください。いつになく恥ずかしがる子どももいれば、いつもの状況とちがうことから不安に思い泣き叫ぶ子もいるかもしれません。
それでも、保護者の皆様にオープンハウスでの参観後、お子様に誇りを感じお帰り頂けることを願っております。

　参観申込書は園入口にあります。参加ご希望日、時間、課程を必ず記入してください。参観は、各家族は一回のみとさせていただきます。参観申し込み締め切りは9月1日金曜日に終了します。それ以降のお申し込みはお受けできませんので予めご理解をお願いいたします。ご協力ありがとうございます。

　　　　　　　ヤマダ園長

 Section II

Q.51　How often is Open House held?

オープンハウスを行う頻度はどのぐらいですか？

1.　　It is a one-time only event.

2.　　It is once a term event.

3.　　It is a once a year event.

4.　　It is a twice a year event.

正解　　4

解説　　4.[It is a twice a year event.(年 2 回のイベントです)] が正解です。

Q.52　Which of the following WON'T parents be able to do at Open House?

保護者がオープンハウスで出来ないことは以下の中どれですか？

1.　　Observe their children's classes.

2.　　Sign up for multiple days.

3.　　Participate in activities with their children.

4.　　Gain insights into their child's development.

正解　　2

解説　　2.[Sign up for multiple days.(複数日の参観申し込み)] が正解です。

Q.53　What does the letter NOT warn about child's behavior?

文書で子どもたちの態度について注意していないことは何ですか？

1.　　Children may get overly excited.

2.　　Children may be uncharacteristically shy.

3.　　Children may become anxious.

4.　　Children may cry.

正解　　1

解説　　1.[Children may get overly excited.(子どもたちが過度に興奮するかもしれない)」
が正解です。

Q.54　What will happen in the event of a late signup for Open House?

オープンハウスに遅れて参観申し込みをした場合どうなりますか？

1.　Late signups will be accommodated if spaces space allow allows.

2.　Late signups will be given the lowest priority for bookings.

3.　Late signups are not accepted at all.

4.　There is no deadline for signups as it is an open campus event.

正解　　3

解説　　3.[Late signups are not accepted at all.(遅い参観申し込みは受付されない)] が正解です。

Q.55　From the letter, what do you feel is the main purpose of Open House?

手紙の内容から、オープンハウスの主目的は何だと感じますか？

1.　To help market the school to families.

2.　To give parents a chance to evaluate teachers.

3.　To give parent a chance to evaluate the school's programs.

4.　To create an opportunity to for parents to experience school life with their children.

正解　　4

解説　　4.[To create an opportunity to for parents to experience school life with their children.(保護者が子どもたちと一緒に園生活を体験する機会をつくる)] が正解です。

 Section II

Listening Passage 2　Q.56-Q.60
ヤマダ園長からキッズ・パティオ園の保護者への手足口病発生についてのお知らせ

Dear Kids Patio Families,

　We would like to inform you that one of our students has a confirmed case of Hand, Foot and Mouth Disease. We also have two unconfirmed cases waiting to be checked by doctors. We would like to advise all families to check your children for symptoms of this disease.

The symptoms are as follows:

• fever

• headache

• fatigue

• rash around the mouth, hands, or feet

• loss of appetite

• diarrhea

　This disease is common during the summer months and can spread through coughing, feces or coming into contact with objects infected with the disease. It also spreads easily at pools. Since we have been doing swim trips throughout the summer, our children may be at high risk of infection.

　We will complete a full body check of all children today and will share our findings at pickup.

　We will also be conducting a thorough cleansing and sanitization of the facility today after the students have left for the day.

Sincerely,

Principal Yamada

キッズ・パティオ園保護者各位

　園児の１人より手足口病が確認されました。また、医師からの確認待ちの園児２人がいます。保護者の皆様にはこの病気の症状についてお子様に確認をお願いいたします。

その症状とは：

・熱

・頭痛

・だるさ

・口手足周りの発疹

・食欲減退

・下痢

　この病気は夏月に発生することが通常で、咳、便、あるいはこの病気で汚染された物からの接触により感染します。また、プールでは簡単に感染します。園では夏の間、他施設での水泳教室を実施しましたので、園児が感染する危険が高いかもしれません。

　本日中に全児童の身体検査を実施します。結果についてはおかえりの際にこちらよりお伝えします。

　また、本日園児の下校後に園施設の完全洗浄、消毒を行います。

ヤマダ園長

Q.56　What will the school do in response to the problem?

問題に対応して園は何をしますか？

1.　　　Stop children from going on pool trips for the rest of the Summer.

2.　　　Send all children to the school nurse for official medical confirmation.

3.　　　Temporarily shut down the school.

4.　　　Clean and sanitize the school.

正解　　4

解説　　4.[Clean and sanitize the school.（学校を洗浄し消毒する）] が正解です。

Q.57　How many cases of Hand Foot and Mouth Disease are there currently at Kids Patio?

現在、キッズ・パティオ園で手足口病にかかっているのは何人いますか？

1.　　　One confirmed case.

2.　　　Two confirmed cases.

3.　　　Three confirmed cases.

4.　　　One confirmed case and two case cases yet to be confirmed.

正解　　4

解説　　4.[One confirmed case and two cases to be confirmed（確認された1名と現在確認中の2名）] が正解です。

Q.58　Which of the following is NOT a symptom of the disease?

病気の兆候ではないのは以下の中、どれですか？

1.　　　Dry mouth

2.　　　Fever

3.　　　Headache

4.　　　Fatigue

正解　　1

解説　　1.[Dry mouth(口の渇き)] は触れられていませんので正解です。

 Section II

Q.59　According to the letter, why are Kids Patio students particularly at risk for the disease?
手紙によれば、特にキッズ・パティオ園の園児たちがこの病気にかかるリスクがある理由は
何ですか？

1. Due to their age.

2. Since they have been doing swim trips all Summer.

3. Due to children's reluctance to wash their hands.

4. Due to poor sanitization standards at the school.

正解　　　2

解説　　　2.[Since they have been doing swim trips all Summer.(夏の間、他施設で水泳教室
をやっているから)] です。

Q.60　According to the letter how long should infected children be kept out of school?
この手紙によると、感染した子どもをどのくらいの期間学校を休ませますか？

1.　　　Children may still attend school even post infection.

2.　　　For a period of one week.

3.　　　Until all blisters have healed and scabbed.

4.　　　This information was not provided in the letter.

正解　　　4

解説　　　4.[This information was not provided in the letter.(この情報はレターには書かれて
いない。)」 が正解です。

 Section II

Listening Passage 3　Q.61-Q.66

An Explanation of Differentiation 差異化について

All children are different. They have different dreams, styles of learning, and abilities. This uniqueness is something that should be both celebrated and planned for.

Differentiation is respecting each child as individual and scaling lesson content to each child's ability. For example, for reading lessons, it's not a good idea to have all children read the same book. Some children may find the book overly challenging, while others may become bored because it is too easy. Instead, assess each child with a leveled reading program and assign books according to their reading level.

Other strategies for differentiation are assigning children to ability-based teams so all lesson content is easily scalable, utilizing a quiz show with various difficulty levels, or organizing small academic workshops where children can challenge materials at their own pace. Even homework assignments can be differentiated. Each child can be sent homework that targets an area of weakness specific to them, which helps to standardize the levels in the class over time.

全ての子どもは違います。皆違う夢、学習のやり方そして能力を持っています。この個性は称賛されるべきものであり、いかされるべきものです。

差異化とは個々の子どもを個人として尊敬し、学習内容を個々の子どもの能力に合わせて作成するものです。例えば、読書の授業では、全ての子どもに同じ本を読ませるのは良い考えではありません。ある子どもにとっては、その本が難しすぎるかもしれず、他の子どもにはやさしすぎて飽きてしまうかもしれません。その代わりに、レベル分けしてある読書プログラムレベルで子どものレベルを調べ、レベルに合った本を与えるようにします。

差異化の他の対策としては、全ての学習内容が容易に測れるようになり子どもを能力に応じたチームに配属したり、様々な難度水準のクイズを活用したり、子ども達が自身のペースで題材に挑戦できる小さなアカデミックワークショップを設けるなどがあります。宿題の出し方でも区別できます。個々の子どもの特に弱い分野に的をしぼった宿題をあたえることで、クラスの水準を時間と共に標準化するのに役立ちます。

 Section II

Q.61 According to the passage, why is differentiation important in the classroom?

パッセージから、なぜ教室内での差異化が重要なのですか？

1. It's a required technique for all certified teachers.

2. Because all children are inherently different.

3. It's statistically proven to improve test scores.

4. Parents demand differentiation in schools.

正解　2

解説　2.[Because all children are inherently different.(なぜなら、全ての子どもは生まれつき違うからです)] が正解です。

Q.62 What do you think the author means by the term "scaling lesson content"?

"学習内容を測る" という著者の言葉の意味は何だと思いますか？

1. Weighing lesson content and only choosing the most effective content.

2. Carefully measuring each student's progress on lesson content.

3. Changing lesson content according to student ability.

4. Always making sure that lesson content is getting progressively more difficult.

正解　3

解説　3.[Changing lesson content according to student ability.(生徒の能力に応じて学習内容を変える)」 が正解です。

Q.63 According to the passage what is the ideal way to host a reading lesson?

パッセージによれば、読書学習を行う上で理想的な方法は何ですか？

1. Have all children read the same book.

2. Have the teacher read a book and the students follow along.

3. Allow children to select a favorite book and read as a group.

4. Assess children's reading level and assign a book based on their level.

正解　4

解説　4.[Assess children's reading level and assign a book based on their level.(子どもの読書レベルを評価し、その水準に基づいた本を与える)]が正解です。

Q.64　What does the passage note as a benefit of differentiated homework?
パッセージは、差異化された宿題の恩恵として何を示していますか？

1.　It helps to standardize student ability over time.

2.　It dramatically improves memory retention.

3.　It improves student test scores.

4.　It makes the process of homework more enjoyable.

正解　1

解説　1.[It helps to standardize student ability over time.（生徒の能力を時間と共に標準化するのに役立ちます）] で、本文で述べられていますから正解です。

Q.65　Which of the following was not mentioned in the passage as a differentiation strategy?
差異化の対策としてパッセージで述べられていないのは以下の中どれですか？

1.　Assigning children to ability-based teams.

2.　Utilizing a quiz show game.

3.　Make sure each activity has three levels of challenge.

4.　Setting up small academic workshop areas.

正解　3

解説　3.[Make sure each activity has three levels of challenge.（各活動が3段階の課題を必ず持つようにすること）] の記述は無いので正解です。

Q.66　Based on what you learned from the passage, what is a likely consequence of not differentiating in the classroom?
パッセージから学んだことに基づけば、教室で差異化しない場合にどのような結果になりますか？

1.　The school will be unable to maintain its accreditation.

2.　Parents will lose confidence in the school.

3.　Students overall test scores will drop.

4.　Students may find lesson content overly difficult or easy.

正解　4

解説　4.[Students may find lesson content overly difficult or easy.（生徒によって学習内容が難しすぎたり、やさしすぎたりします。）] が正解です。

幼保 英語検定

幼保英語検定

案内

幼保英語検定受検案内

受検級	4級から1級まで5つの級
受検資格	不問です。　※いずれの級からも受検可
検定開催	年に3回に実施。個人受検と団体受検があり
	春季検定　7月　第3日曜日
	秋季検定　11月　第3日曜日
	初春検定　2月　第3日曜日
	※1級は、年1回春季検定7月第3日曜日のみ実施
申込方法	協会のホームページからのインターネット申込
申込期間	前検定開催日翌日から次回検定開催日の属する月前月の第4日曜日翌日まで
	隣接した2つの級の併願申込可。(同一日、同一会場が条件です)
受 検 料	4級　3,500円　3級　4,000円　　2級　4,500円　準1級　6,500円＊(二次1回目を含みます)1級　7,000円＊(二次1回目を含みます)

協会ホームページ受検案内

https://www.youhoeigo.com/guidance/overview.html

準1級レベルの出題区分

配点、出題形式などはこちらでご確認ください。
https://www.youhoeigo.com/guidance/pg3150741.html

幼保 英語検定

資格証について

資格証の案内

幼保英語士資格証付与について

幼保教育・保育英語検定（幼保英語検定）に合格した人材であることを明示するため、資格証の付与を下記の要領で行います。

対象：幼保英語検定　4級、3級、2級、準1級、1級　検定合格者

資格呼称：　幼保英語士資格証

幼保英語検定　4級	Level：Introductory
幼保英語検定　3級	Level：Beginner
幼保英語検定　2級	Level：Intermediate
幼保英語検定　準1級	Level：Advances
幼保英語検定　1級	Level：Proficiency

有効期間：

合格した検定の一般公開記念日から3年後の対応する検定日前日まで有効とします。

資格の更新：　有効期限満了日もしくは直前実施の検定を受検し合格すること。

4級、3級、2級：	再受験
準1級、1級：	二次試験のみ再受験（※更新の際の受験料は3,000円）

申請方法：

幼保教育・保育英語検定協会ホームページの「幼保英語士資格証付与について」から申込

発行費用：

1)新規申請：2,000円

2)更新申請：2,000円

　　　　無断転載・複写を禁じます

提出写真規格：こちら<u>https://www.youhoeigo.com/certificate/about_photo.html</u>から確認

提出写真規格について

申込書：オンライン上にてフォームに入力

支払方法：クレジットカード、コンビニ、銀行もしくは郵便局でお支払いください。

資格証詳細・申込はこちらから

一般社団法人 幼児教育・保育英語検定協会　　　　準1級

フリガナ	
名前	

保 有 資 格	有	無
保育士	①	②
幼稚園教諭	①	②
小学校教諭	①	②
中高校教諭	①	②
介護福祉士	①	②
看護師	①	②
ヘルパー	①	②
栄養士	①	②
海外の保育資格	①	②

(有:見込みを含む)

受検番号

①①①①①①①①①①①
②②②②②②②②②②②
③③③③③③③③③③③
④④④④④④④④④④④
⑤⑤⑤⑤⑤⑤⑤⑤⑤⑤⑤
⑥⑥⑥⑥⑥⑥⑥⑥⑥⑥⑥
⑦⑦⑦⑦⑦⑦⑦⑦⑦⑦⑦
⑧⑧⑧⑧⑧⑧⑧⑧⑧⑧⑧
⑨⑨⑨⑨⑨⑨⑨⑨⑨⑨⑨
⑩⑩⑩⑩⑩⑩⑩⑩⑩⑩⑩

マークシート解答記入について

記入方法	1 記入は必ずHBの黒鉛筆で正確に塗りつぶしてください。 2 訂正する場合は、消しゴムできれいに消してください。 3 解答用紙を汚したり、折り曲がったりしないでください。 4 正しく記入（塗りつぶし）されていない場合は読みとれなくなります。	記入例	良い例　● 悪い例　✓ ◉ ⊖

解答欄	
Q.1	①②③④
Q.2	①②③④
Q.3	①②③④
Q.4	①②③④
Q.5	①②③④
Q.6	①②③④
Q.7	①②③④
Q.8	①②③④
Q.9	①②③④
Q.10	①②③④
Q.11	①②③④
Q.12	①②③④
Q.13	①②③④
Q.14	①②③④
Q.15	①②③④
Q.16	①②③④
Q.17	①②③④
Q.18	①②③④
Q.19	①②③④
Q.20	①②③④

① (欄外)

解答欄	
Q.21	①②③④
Q.22	①②③④
Q.23	①②③④
Q.24	①②③④
Q.25	①②③④
Q.26	①②③④
Q.27	①②③④
Q.28	①②③④
Q.29	①②③④
Q.30	①②③④
Q.31	①②③④
Q.32	①②③④
Q.33	①②③④
Q.34	①②③④
Q.35	①②③④
Q.36	①②③④
Q.37	①②③④
Q.38	①②③④
Q.39	①②③④
Q.40	①②③④

② ③ (欄外)

解答欄

④ Q.41　（英作文）
この用紙の裏面に記入

リスニング　解答欄

⑤	Q.42	①②③④
	Q.43	①②③④
	Q.44	①②③④
	Q.45	①②③④
	Q.46	①②③④

リスニング　解答欄

⑤	Q.47	①②③④
	Q.48	①②③④
	Q.49	①②③④
	Q.50	①②③④
	Q.51	①②③④
	Q.52	①②③④
	Q.53	①②③④
	Q.54	①②③④
	Q.55	①②③④
	Q.56	①②③④
	Q.57	①②③④
	Q.58	①②③④
	Q.59	①②③④
	Q.60	①②③④
	Q.61	①②③④
	Q.62	①②③④
	Q.63	①②③④
	Q.64	①②③④
	Q.65	①②③④
	Q.66	①②③④

Section IV   Writing

Q.41

_____

_____

_____

_____

_____

_____

(30 words)

score	

一般社団法人 幼児教育・保育英語検定協会　　　**準1級**

フリガナ	
名前	

保　有　資　格	有	無
保育士	①	②
幼稚園教諭	①	②
小学校教諭	①	②
中高校教諭	①	②
介護福祉士	①	②
看護師	①	②
ヘルパー	①	②
栄養士	①	②
海外の保育資格	①	②

(有:見込みを含む)

受検番号

① ① ① ① ① ① ① ① ① ①
② ② ② ② ② ② ② ② ② ②
③ ③ ③ ③ ③ ③ ③ ③ ③ ③
④ ④ ④ ④ ④ ④ ④ ④ ④ ④
⑤ ⑤ ⑤ ⑤ ⑤ ⑤ ⑤ ⑤ ⑤ ⑤
⑥ ⑥ ⑥ ⑥ ⑥ ⑥ ⑥ ⑥ ⑥ ⑥
⑦ ⑦ ⑦ ⑦ ⑦ ⑦ ⑦ ⑦ ⑦ ⑦
⑧ ⑧ ⑧ ⑧ ⑧ ⑧ ⑧ ⑧ ⑧ ⑧
⑨ ⑨ ⑨ ⑨ ⑨ ⑨ ⑨ ⑨ ⑨ ⑨
⓪ ⓪ ⓪ ⓪ ⓪ ⓪ ⓪ ⓪ ⓪ ⓪

マークシート解答記入について

記入方法	1 記入は必ずHBの黒鉛筆で正確に塗りつぶしてください。 2 訂正する場合は、消しゴムできれいに消してください。 3 解答用紙を汚したり、折り曲がったりしないでください。 4 正しく記入(塗りつぶし)されていない場合は読みとれなくなります。	記入例	良い例　● 悪い例　✓ ◉ ⊖

解答欄	
Q1	①②③④
Q2	①②③④
Q3	①②③④
Q4	①②③④
Q5	①②③④
Q6	①②③④
Q7	①②③④
Q8	①②③④
Q9	①②③④
Q10	①②③④
Q11	①②③④
Q12	①②③④
Q13	①②③④
Q14	①②③④
Q15	①②③④
Q16	①②③④
Q17	①②③④
Q18	①②③④
Q19	①②③④
Q20	①②③④

(①)

解答欄	
Q21	①②③④
Q22	①②③④
Q23	①②③④
Q24	①②③④
Q25	①②③④
Q26	①②③④
Q27	①②③④
Q28	①②③④
Q29	①②③④
Q30	①②③④
Q31	①②③④
Q32	①②③④
Q33	①②③④
Q34	①②③④
Q35	①②③④
Q36	①②③④
Q37	①②③④
Q38	①②③④
Q39	①②③④
Q40	①②③④

(② Q21–Q30)　(③ Q31–Q40)

解答欄

④ Q41 （英作文） この用紙の裏面に記入

リスニング　解答欄

Q42	①②③④
Q43	①②③④
Q44	①②③④
Q45	①②③④
Q46	①②③④

(⑤)

リスニング　解答欄

Q47	①②③④
Q48	①②③④
Q49	①②③④
Q50	①②③④
Q51	①②③④
Q52	①②③④
Q53	①②③④
Q54	①②③④
Q55	①②③④
Q56	①②③④
Q57	①②③④
Q58	①②③④
Q59	①②③④
Q60	①②③④
Q61	①②③④
Q62	①②③④
Q63	①②③④
Q64	①②③④
Q65	①②③④
Q66	①②③④

(⑤)

Section IV   Writing

Q.41

_____

_____

_____

_____

_____

_____

(30 words)

score	

178

表 一般社団法人 幼児教育・保育英語検定協会　　**準1級**

フリガナ	
名前	

保 有 資 格	有	無
保育士	①	②
幼稚園教諭	①	②
小学校教諭	①	②
中高校教諭	①	②
介護福祉士	①	②
看護師	①	②
ヘルパー	①	②
栄養士	①	②
海外の保育資格	①	②

(有:見込みを含む)

受検番号

①①①①①①①①①①①
②②②②②②②②②②②
③③③③③③③③③③③
④④④④④④④④④④④
⑤⑤⑤⑤⑤⑤⑤⑤⑤⑤⑤
⑥⑥⑥⑥⑥⑥⑥⑥⑥⑥⑥
⑦⑦⑦⑦⑦⑦⑦⑦⑦⑦⑦
⑧⑧⑧⑧⑧⑧⑧⑧⑧⑧⑧
⑨⑨⑨⑨⑨⑨⑨⑨⑨⑨⑨
⓪⓪⓪⓪⓪⓪⓪⓪⓪⓪⓪

マークシート解答記入について

記入方法	1 記入は必ずHBの黒鉛筆で正確に塗りつぶしてください。 2 訂正する場合は、消しゴムできれいに消してください。 3 解答用紙を汚したり、折り曲がったりしないでください。 4 正しく記入(塗りつぶし)されていない場合は読みとれなくなります。	記入例	良い例　● 悪い例　✓ ◉ ⊖

解答欄 ①

Q1	①②③④
Q2	①②③④
Q3	①②③④
Q4	①②③④
Q5	①②③④
Q6	①②③④
Q7	①②③④
Q8	①②③④
Q9	①②③④
Q10	①②③④
Q11	①②③④
Q12	①②③④
Q13	①②③④
Q14	①②③④
Q15	①②③④
Q16	①②③④
Q17	①②③④
Q18	①②③④
Q19	①②③④
Q20	①②③④

解答欄 ② ③

Q21	①②③④
Q22	①②③④
Q23	①②③④
Q24	①②③④
Q25	①②③④
Q26	①②③④
Q27	①②③④
Q28	①②③④
Q29	①②③④
Q30	①②③④
Q31	①②③④
Q32	①②③④
Q33	①②③④
Q34	①②③④
Q35	①②③④
Q36	①②③④
Q37	①②③④
Q38	①②③④
Q39	①②③④
Q40	①②③④

解答欄 ④ ⑤

④ Q41　（英作文）　この用紙の裏面に記入

リスニング　解答欄 ⑤

Q42	①②③④
Q43	①②③④
Q44	①②③④
Q45	①②③④
Q46	①②③④

リスニング 解答欄 ⑤

Q47	①②③④
Q48	①②③④
Q49	①②③④
Q50	①②③④
Q51	①②③④
Q52	①②③④
Q53	①②③④
Q54	①②③④
Q55	①②③④
Q56	①②③④
Q57	①②③④
Q58	①②③④
Q59	①②③④
Q60	①②③④
Q61	①②③④
Q62	①②③④
Q63	①②③④
Q64	①②③④
Q65	①②③④
Q66	①②③④

Section IV   Writing

Q.41

_____

_____

_____

_____

_____

_____

(30 words)

score	

幼保英語検定　準1級ワークブック
2023年6月20初版1刷発行

著者　　　　一般社団法人国際子育て人材支援機構
発行所　　　一般社団法人国際子育て人材支援機構
　　　　　　〒153-0061 東京都目黒区中目黒 3-6-2
　　　　　　Tel 03-5725-0554 Fax 03-6452-4148　　http://www.b-parenting.org
発売所　　　株式会社　ブックフォレ
　　　　　　〒224-0003 神奈川県横浜市都筑区中川中央 1-21-3-2F
　　　　　　Tel 045-910-1020 Fax 045-910-1040　http://www.bookfore.co.jp

印刷・製本　　冊子印刷社

ISBN978-4-909846-54-9